HOME ECONOMICS IN ACTION

TEXTILES

Judith Christian-Carter
and Bridget Crabtree

Oxford University Press 1988

Oxford University Press, Walton Street, Oxford OX2 6DP

Oxford New York Toronto
Delhi Bombay Calcutta Madras Karachi
Petaling Jaya Singapore Hong Kong Tokyo
Nairobi Dar es Salaam Cape Town
Melbourne Auckland

and associated companies in
Beirut Berlin Ibadan Nicosia

Oxford is a trade mark of Oxford University Press

To all our former students,
with fondest memories

Acknowledgements

The publishers would like to thank the following for permission to reproduce photographs:

Bogod Machine Co. Ltd. (Bernina) p.51 (top right and bottom left); Brabantia (UK) Ltd. p.84; Richard Butchins p.68 (all), p.72, p.93; Colorific! p.11 (bottom right); Crafts Council: Susan Bosence p.36 (left), B. Cox p.21; Dylon International Ltd. p.32 (both); David Evans & Co. p.36 (right); Chris Honeywell p.6 (bottom right), p.42; The Hutchison Library p.64 (top right); Jones (and Brother) Sewing Machine Co. Ltd. p.23 (bottom); Rob Judges p.6 (top right and bottom left), p.11 (top left and top middle), p.15 (both), p.16, p.19, p.22 (both), p.23 (top), p.24 (top and bottom), p.28 (all), p.29, p.31, p.34 (both), p.37, p.38, p.39 (both) p.53, p.56 (all), p.57, p.59 (both), p.60, p.61, p.67, p.73, p.74, p.80, p.82 (all), p.87, p.90; The Lace Guild p.24 (middle); Levi Strauss Ltd. p.43; New Home Sewing Machine Co. p.51 (bottom right); Shirley Institute p.14 (all); Simpson Mahoney Parrock (Singer Co. Ltd.) p.51 (top left); Spectrum Colour Library p.6 (top middle and bottom middle), p.8 (right), p.11 (top right, bottom left and bottom middle), p.64 (top middle); Peter Storm p.44 (top); Elizabeth Whiting and Associates p.76, p.78 (left); Zefa Picture Library (UK) Ltd. p.6 (top left), p.8 (left), p.64 (top left, bottom left, bottom middle, bottom right), p.78 (right).

The publishers would also like to thank the following for permission to reproduce their work:

In Stitches; pupils of Oxford College of Further Education; pupils of Park House School, Newbury; pupils of Peers County Secondary School, Oxford; Mrs M. Pope; Mrs V. Rees; and Liberty's.

The illustrations are by Ann Blockley, Sheelagh Bowie, Alan Rowe, Alexa Rutherford, and Jacqui Thomas.

The cover illustration is by Raynor Design.

Designed by Raynor Design.

Set by MS Filmsetting Limited, Frome, Somerset
Printed in Hong Kong

Contents

Introduction   4

1 Taking a look at textiles   6

2 Teasing out the fibres   11

3 Spinning a right old yarn!   17

4 Making fabric   21

5 Colouring fabrics   29

6 Getting print on to fabrics   36

7 And now for the finishing touch!   41

8 One way to sew it up   46

9 Adding an extra bit of something   55

10 The clothes on your back   64

11 The DIY clothes section   70

12 Textiles all around us   76

13 Looking after textiles: keeping them clean   83

14 Looking after textiles: running repairs   91

Introduction

In writing this book for young people aged 11 to 14 we have been given the opportunity to communicate to other teachers of Home Economics many of our ideas and experiences gained over several years of teaching textiles.

The ideas in this book are derived from a variety of sources: from talking to a number of textiles specialists to experiences gained from teaching textiles to students of widely differing abilities and ages. The content of the book reflects what we feel young people aged 11 to 14 need to know about textiles, with the sincere hope that its use will encourage a greater interest in the subject both inside and outside school. We hope that the book may serve to develop new interests for young people and will also give them the confidence to tackle a variety of textile-based problems in the course of their lives.

While the content of this book forms a logical progression through Units 1 to 14, each unit is complete in itself so that units may be taken out of order if desired. The units can be grouped in a variety of ways to suit individual needs although some of the later units are perhaps more relevant to 14-year-olds.

Units 1–4 provide the foundation for an understanding of textiles and serve to introduce a number of basic and essential concepts. Units 5–9 develop a number of the concepts and ideas introduced previously and follow on from previous units. Units 10–14 may be left to a later stage in a course, such as the third year. This is one suggestion for grouping units but should not be regarded as the only way. Indeed, we hope that both teachers and students will use this book in as free a way as possible to suit individual teaching and learning styles; in this way everyone will get the most from it.

The topics included in this book are those which we consider to be the foundations of any course in textiles. It is hoped that the topics will give students a good idea of the meaning of the word 'textiles' and a broader picture of what the subject area is about. It is important to stress that the book is presented as a foundation course which, in itself, implies that students should be encouraged to use other books and to acquire information from difference sources in order to develop their ideas.

Every so often tasks are included for students to do. These are not compulsory by any means, but have been included to stimulate thought and activity and to develop previous learning. All tasks have been coded so that teachers and students may see in advance the nature of the task:

 indicates a task involving thinking and writing;

 indicates a task involving practical textile work;

 indicates a task involving investigation and testing;

 indicates a task involving planning and drawing.

The content of this book reflects very strongly our belief that Home Economics is essentially a problem-solving activity. The process of problem solving and the learning processes which can be fostered through the medium of textiles are the foundations upon which this book is based.

There are several ways in which any problem in Home Economics can be solved and we are aware that many schools will be using their own system. However, most of these methods are composed of the same few, key, steps, and we hope that the approach reflected in this book will fit neatly into any system currently being used.

We hope that teachers and students will enjoy using this book and working with textiles and that such use will pave the way to further work and a greater interest in this area.

Judith Christian-Carter
Bridget Crabtree
January 1987

UNIT 1

Taking a look at textiles

What are textiles?

Textiles is a word that a lot of people use, but do they know what it means?

 Have a good look at the pictures above.
What do they all have in common? ☐

All the people in the pictures are wearing clothes. Their clothes are made of **fabrics**. Because their clothes are made of fabrics we can say that they are wearing **textile items**. And because all the other things in the pictures, like the toy and the cushion, are made of fabrics, these are textile items too.

 Now, look again at the pictures and list all the textile items you can see. ☐

Textiles are all around us

 Have a look around you. What textile items can you see in the room? □

Draw ten textile items that you would find in your living room at home. Label each item that you draw so you will remember what it is. Check your drawings with another person in the class. Is there anything which you had not thought of? □

Think back to your last summer holiday. List ten textile items you came into contact with on your holiday. □

Now draw a simple house and label the rooms.
Take each room you have labelled and make a list of all the textile items you can think of which could be found in that room.
Remember – you already have ten items for the living room. □

What about outside the home? How many places can you think of where you might find textiles being used?
Try using these headings to help you:
sport – hospitals – on the beach – transport – school. □

Once you start to think about it you can see how textiles are all around us. But what about you?

Draw a match-stick person and label all the things made out of textiles which could be found on that person.

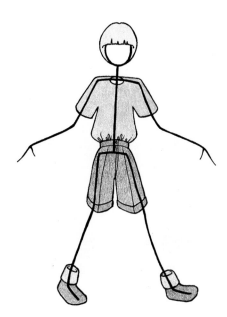

How many things have you labelled? □

By now you have probably discovered that textile items can be made from all sorts of different fabrics. These fabrics can be soft, hard, thick, thin, firm, or holey. When fabrics are made into something, then we have a textile item.

How do you know which fabrics to choose?

If you want to choose a suitable fabric for an item, then it's a great help to know something about fabrics. For example, what is each fabric made from, how has it been made, and what are its special features or properties? If you want to choose fabric for a cushion cover, or buy a sail for a boat, a shirt for school, or some motorcycling gear, then it's a good idea to know what to look out for.

 What properties do you think are important for the following textile items:
a bath towel; a parachute; a tent; an all-in-one ski suit? □

If you found this a bit difficult, don't worry. We will start at the very beginning so that you can see what it's all about.

Taking a closer look

The first thing to realize is that textile items are very different from one another. They need to be different because we use them for different things. The fabric which is used to make a sail is very different from the fabric used to make a sports shirt. This is because different items need different **properties** if they are going to be of any use to us.

Just imagine a sports shirt which did not absorb your sweat. There you are running around, getting really hot. Because your shirt won't absorb your sweat it runs down your body – there must be nicer ways of getting wet! So **absorbency** can be a very important property. On the other hand, a sail on a boat needs to be non-absorbent and flexible. If it was stretchy, just think how slowly you would go!

Other properties which may be important for different textile items are:
- how easily the item burns (flammability);
- how resistant to stains it is (stain resistance);
- how easily it shrinks (shrinkage);
- how hardwearing it is;
- how resistant it is to creases (crease resistance);
- how easily it keeps creases or pleats (crease holding);
- how warm it is;
- how smooth it is;
- how stretchy it is;
- whether its shape has been set by heat (e.g pleats and creases).

 What do you think are the **two** most important properties of the following items:

a jumper for you to wear to school;
a net for catching fish in;
a swimsuit or swimming trunks;
curtains in a bathroom;
a hot air balloon;
a fireperson's suit? □

The various ways in which textile items are made and the fabrics used to make them all help to give textile items different properties.

Taking textiles apart

 Find a piece of hessian measuring about 10 cm × 10 cm. You will also need a hand lens and two mounted needles. Try the following:

1 Take a good look at the fabric. Don't use the lens at this stage. Can you see lots of strands twisted or interlaced together?
2 Now have a look at the fabric using the hand lens. The strands should be much clearer.
3 Pull one of these strands. These strands are also called **threads** or lengths of **yarn**.
   Have a look at this strand under the hand lens. Can you see what it is made of?
4 Now see if you can pull the strand apart. Try untwisting the yarn to get a very fine, wispy piece. This is called a **fibre**. Hold on to the fibre very carefully and look at it under the hand lens. What does it look like?
   Make sure that you have only one fibre as they are very tightly twisted together. Use the mounted needles to pull them apart.
5 Mount all your samples on some paper or in a book. You should have a sample of:
   fabric;
   thread/yarn;
   fibre. □

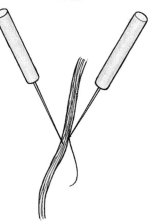

How tiny is your fibre?

Have a closer look at the fibre. See how very tiny it is? It is like a hair to look at. To know where these fibres come from is important. Thousands of them are put together in many different ways to make a fabric. If we know where they come from then we can make sure that we use them, wear them, and look after them properly.

Another look at this unit

1 Textile items are all around us.

2 Textile items are the clothes we wear and all items made from fabrics that we use inside and outside the home.

3 The study of textiles involves looking at fabrics and how they are made from fibres, as well as making items for yourself and others to use or to wear.

4 Textile items need different properties to do the jobs they are designed for. Some need to be absorbent, some stretchy, some hardwearing, and so on.

5 Textile items are made from fabrics. Fabrics are made from yarns and fibres.

UNIT 2

Teasing out the fibres

Fibres – the smallest part

Have a good look at the pictures above. What do you think they have got in common?

It's not that easy to see the link but there is one. They are all used to make fibres! Some of these fibres are short and are known as **staple fibres**. Other fibres are very long and are called **continuous filaments**. The length of the fibre is important because different fabrics and textile items can be made from different lengths of fibres.

There are many different types of fibres. To make life easier we can put fibres into three groups depending on where they come from.

Group one: natural fibres

All these fibres comes from nature, i.e. from animals or vegetables. Silk comes from the cocoon of a silk worm. Silk is a continuous filament. Wool comes from the coat of sheep. It is a staple fibre. Both silk and wool are animal fibres.

Vegetable fibres come from plants. Cotton and flax are vegetable fibres. Cotton is a staple fibre and the fibres are found inside a ripened cotton boll. Flax is also a staple fibre but here the fibres are found inside the stalks of the plant.

Yarn made from continuous filament fibres

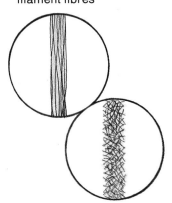

Yarn made from staple fibres

Group two: man-made fibres

This group of fibres comes from nature but has chemicals added to it. Viscose, acetate, and triacetate rayon are examples of fibres made in this way. For example, viscose rayon fibres come from spruce trees. The trees are cut up into logs and then shredded into wood chips. The wood chips are then mixed with chemicals and spun to make fibres.

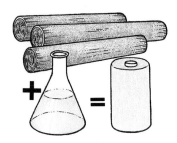

Group three: synthetic fibres

These fibres are made entirely from chemicals. Synthetic fibres include the polyamides (e.g. nylon), polyesters, and acrylics. For example, nylon fibres come from oil or coal which has been mixed with water, air, and certain chemicals.

Because man-made fibres and synthetic fibres aren't found in nature they can be made either as staple fibres or as continuous filaments. This is rather handy as we shall see later.

What are you wearing today?

Have a look at the clothes you are wearing. Check the labels to see what your clothes are made of. You don't have to take all your clothes off to do this!
Make a chart, like the one below, and fill it in.

GARMENT	FIBRES USED	FIBRE GROUP
Blouse/shirt	50% cotton	Natural
	50% polyester	Synthetic
Skirt/trousers		
Jumper/cardigan		
Tie		
Blazer/jacket		

Try and add some more textile items to this list when you get home and get undressed. Have a look at any other items, such as a towel, that you might use before you go to bed.
Did you remember to see what your socks were made of? ▢

Taking a closer look

To take a closer look you will need to use a microscope. A microscope may have several lenses going from low power ($\times 10$) to much higher power ($\times 100$).

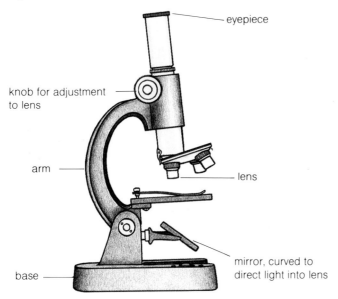

This is one way to use a microscope:
1 Switch on the light bulb fitted into the base.
2 Put a slide on the microscope stage.
3 Put the low-power lens under the eyepiece.
4 Turn the focusing knob so that the low-power lens is close to the slide.
5 Adjust the focusing knob to give a clear picture. Move the slide if you want to see another part of the item.
6 To see more detail use a higher-powered lens.

Looking at fibres

 You will need:
● fabric samples of wool, silk, cotton, polyamide, viscose rayon, acetate rayon, polyester, and acrylic
● two mounted needles
● for each sample: slides
cover slips
water in a pipette
a dark background (to place the slide on so that you can see the fibre).

Taking one sample at a time:
1 Place a slide on a dark background. Place a short length of the yarn on the slide and pull apart using the mounted needles.
2 Put one or two drops of water on to the fibres using the pipette.
3 Cover the fibres with a cover slip.
4 Look at the fibres though the microscope. ▢

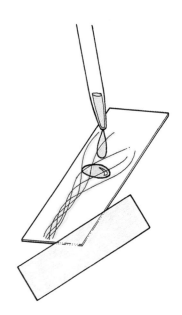

What do your fibres look like?

Do the fibres look anything like the ones in these pictures?

Wool: notice the scales on each staple fibre.

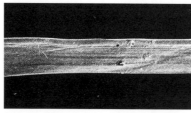

Silk: these continuous filaments are long and smooth.

Cotton: these staple fibres are like ribbons and are twisted.

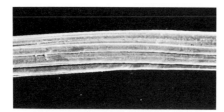

Viscose: a continuous filament which looks like a long, serrated rod.

Polyester: a continuous filament which is long, round, and rod-like.

Putting it all together

All fibres look very different. Not only do they look very different but they also have different properties or characteristics. The properties that a fibre has come about because of its shape; for example, wool is warm because of its scales. Here are some fibres and the properties that they have:

Wool   The scales on these fibres trap air. Still air is a good insulator. Woollen clothing keeps you warm because the heat from your body cannot escape. The still air in the fibres stops the heat from your body going anywhere. Wool is also very absorbent and stretchy. This can be a problem sometimes, for example when jumpers stretch that little bit too much! Moths love wool which means that the fibres can get nibbled and holes appear. Also, if you don't wash wool carefully it will matt because the scales (see photo) rub and lock together which makes them shrink in size. Wool can also be a bit on the pricey side.

Silk   Silk fibres can make a very shiny fabric which hangs well. Silk is strong and absorbent; it is also light to wear and it keeps you warm. It colours or dyes easily but it is expensive because there is not very much of it around. It takes one silk worm a long time to spin enough silk to make just a small handkerchief!

Cotton   This is very absorbent, soft, and smooth. It is very strong and is even stronger when it is wet. It washes well but it does crease very easily. It's great for sportswear as it also feels cool to wear.

Viscose   This too is absorbent. It doesn't shrink but it does crease easily. It is also much weaker when it is wet. It colours or dyes well.

Polyamides **Nylon** is an example of a polyamide. Polyamides are very strong, but not very absorbent. This means that they repel water well which makes them ideal for coats and jackets. They don't shrink. They do attract dirt because they produce quite a lot of static electricity. This means that the fibre has an electric charge which attracts dirt, in much the same way as a comb which you have rubbed on your sleeve can make your hair stand on end!

Polyesters These are strong, not very absorbent, and don't shrink. They are also crease resistant and if you try to crease them you will find that they recover well. They can also be heat set which means that you can make pleats or creases, set them in place by heating, then they are there for ever. They are often called 'easy-care' fabrics because they don't need much attention.

Acrylics These are soft and warm to the touch. Some can look like wool but are not nearly so expensive! They are also light in weight, easy to wash, and can be heat set. They are not very absorbent and don't crease easily but they are quite strong and dry well.

Doing a little bit of testing

Have a go at testing out some properties for yourself.

Looking at absorbency Take a 10 cm square of cotton, wool, polyester, and acrilan. Use a pipette and drop a droplet of water on each of the fabrics. Watch what happens to the water. What conclusions do you come to?

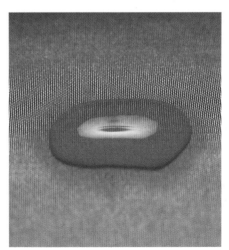

Attracting dirt See if you can rub two pieces of polyester together and attract dirt with the static electricity you produce. Why is dirt attracted by static electricity? ☐

Now see if you can think of a way to compare how hardwearing cotton, wool, and polyester are. When you have done this try to compare how warm cotton, wool, and polyester are to wear. ☐

Mixing up your fibres!

When a fabric is made from fibres, the fabric will have the same properties or characteristics as the fibres which were used to make it. But when different fibres are mixed together or **blended** to make a fabric, the fabric then has all the good properties of the fibres with less of the not so good properties, which is pretty clever stuff! A lot of the fabrics we use today have many different properties because they are made of several different fibres. For example, polyester and cotton are often used together to make shirts. Shirts made from polyester and cotton have all the good properties of polyester and cotton together. They are strong, cool, absorbent, and they wear well; don't crease easily, and are easy to look after.

Polyester/cotton   Cotton

Something for you to do

 Draw a clothes line full of clothes.
Label each garment with: its name; its fibre content; and the properties of the fibres that make them suitable for that garment (use this unit to help you). □

You may have noticed that the fibre content is often the same for lots of different items but that the actual items can look very different from each other. We will look at the reasons for this in another unit.

Another look at this unit

1 Fibres are tiny hair-like strands that can be twisted together to form a yarn or thread.
2 Different fibres have different properties.
3 Knowing where fibres come from helps us to understand what properties various fabrics have. The shape and composition of the fibres used in a fabric give that fabric certain properties.
4 Fibres can be put into three main groups: natural – from nature; man-made – from nature and mixed with chemicals; and synthetics – just from chemicals.

UNIT 3

Spinning a right old yarn!

Why do we need yarns?

We need to make some fibres into yarns first before they can be made into fabrics. You can take some fibres and make them into fabrics straight away, but with other fibres you can't do this because they wouldn't look like fabrics at all. For example, disposable dish cloths are made straight from fibres, while jeans are made from yarn.

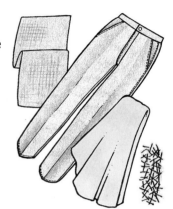

 Which kind of fabric do you think lasts longer and wears better:
(a) fabric made directly from fibres, or,
(b) fabric made from yarns which are made from fibres?
Which kind of fabric do you think would be the cheapest?
Explain your answer. □

Putting fibres together

We can put fibres into two groups depending on how long they are:
1 Short fibres, such as those found in cotton, flax, and wool, are called **staple fibres** (see Unit 2 p. 11).
2 Long fibres, such as those from cultivated silk but not wild silk, are called **continuous filaments**.

 See if you can find out why the fibres from wild silk are shorter than the fibres from cultivated silk. ■

Just as natural fibres can be either staple fibres or continuous filaments, so too can man-made and synthetic fibres. Depending on which type is wanted the manufacturer simply makes the fibres either long or short.

Now have a go at making your own yarn:
Take a small ball of cotton wool.
Have a close look at the cotton wool – do you see that it is just a lot of tiny fibres?
Now try to make it into a yarn – pull it gently and twist with your fingers.
Look at your yarn. Is it really even in width? If it is then you have done very well. □

Getting into a right old spin!

In fact what you have done is a little simple spinning. Spinning is just pulling and twisting fibres together to form yarn. This type of yarn is known as simple yarn. Different types of yarn can be made though by using different fibres and different methods of spinning.

 See if you can have a go at spinning wool fibres using a spindle.□

spun yarn

spindle

Making yarns today

Yarns are made by machines and several different methods are used. Depending on what fibre is used and what sort of yarn is produced different fabrics will be produced. The fabrics will differ in what they look like, how they wear, and how comfortable they feel.

Putting in a bit of a twist

As fibres are made into yarns they are twisted. This twisting holds the fibres together. The more twist the stronger the yarn.

 Find a piece of cheap string.
Look at how it is already twisted.
Now carry on twisting it. Does it make it stronger?
Carry on twisting and twisting the string until it curls back on itself.
Is this stronger than before?
Continue twisting it and see if you can make it break.□

So, a loose twist gives a softer but thicker yarn which is not as strong as a yarn which has been twisted a lot more. A loose twist also means that you can pull the yarn apart far more easily than with a more twisted yarn.

If the fibres are twisted from left to right then the yarn has an 'S' twist. If the fibres are twisted from right to left then the yarn has a 'Z' twist. By twisting fibres in these two different ways different types of yarn can be made.

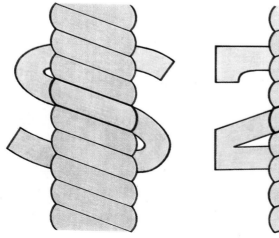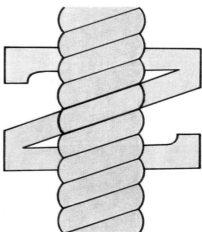

What happens with even more twisting?

Well, by twisting more than one simple yarn together a **ply** yarn is made. So the names 'two-ply' and 'four-ply' wool tell you how many yarns the wool has twisted together. However, the twisting of each yarn must be done in the opposite direction to the other yarns, otherwise the whole thing would untwist and knot up.

 Think about what the name 'plywood' means. What do plywood and ply yarn have in common? □

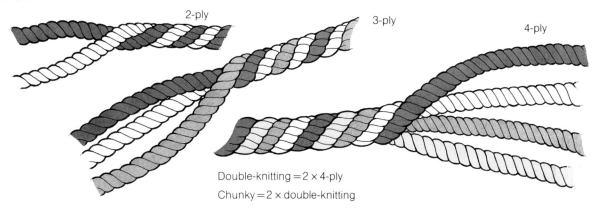

Double-knitting = 2 × 4-ply
Chunky = 2 × double-knitting

The other thing about giving a yarn a lot of twist is that it helps to make a rough texture to the finished fabric. For example, crepe yarns have a lot of twist in them so that the yarn curls up (just like it did with the piece of string). This gives a rough texture to the crepe fabric.

Other twists on a yarn!

Some very complex yarns can be made today. They all have different appearances depending on how they were made.

Crepe

For example, some parts of the yarn can be left untwisted (this is known as slub yarn); some extra small fibres can be added into the twist of the yarn (e.g. flock and chenille yarns); one yarn can be wrapped round another but with a looser twist giving a knobbed effect (called bouclé yarn); and two or more different yarns can be twisted together (grandrelle yarns).

It's not important to remember all these different names. What is important is that you realize how different fabrics are made. As people experiment more with fibres and yarns it is likely that we shall be able to buy and use an even greater variety of fabrics.

 Have a look at the structure of a number of different yarns under a hand lens. See if you can spot the major differences.
Collect a number of different yarns. Arrange them into a pleasing design or shape by sticking them on to a piece of cardboard. How many types of yarn have you used? Can you name some of them? □

Blending fibres

Sometimes manufacturers want certain properties in a fabric. They get these by spinning together two different fibres to make a yarn. This is called **blending**. In this way the best properties of the two fibres are used to make an even better fabric (e.g. polyester and cotton are spun together to make blouses and shirts: see Unit 2 p. 16).

 See if you can find out what other blends are used to make fabrics for clothes. Try to find another three blends and then work out why the fibres used in each blend have been chosen. It might help if you have a look at some textile items (e.g. clothes) in the shops. ▢

Adding some texture

Remember that some synthetic fibres can be set by heat (p. 9). In technical terms, they are **thermoplastic**. This means that manufacturers are now able to make a lot of synthetic fibres look and feel like a number of natural fibres. They do this by adding 'bulk' to the synthetic yarns which makes them stretch well. Adding bulk also makes them warmer to wear because of the air which gets trapped in this process. The process is called **texturing** and yarns made in this way are called **textured yarns**.

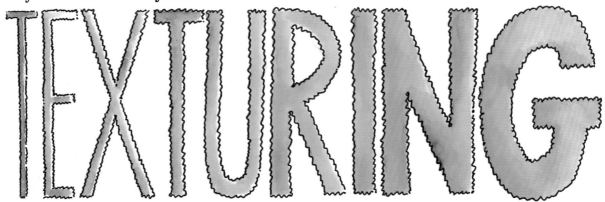

In this way lots of different fabrics can be made which are often cheaper than their natural look-alikes.

> ### Another look at this unit
> 1 Simple yarn can be made by pulling and twisting the fibres into an even width. This is called **spinning**.
> 2 **Twisting** the yarn makes it stronger. By twisting the yarn in different directions different types of yarn can be made.
> 3 Two different fibres can be twisted together to make a yarn. This is called **blending**. In this way the good properties of both fibres are found in the fabric produced from the yarn.
> 4 **Texturing** makes yarns from synthetic fibres more like those yarns from natural fibres.

UNIT 4

Making fabrics

There are many different ways of making fabrics out of fibres and yarns.

How many ways of making fabrics can you think of?
Have a good look at some of the clothes you are wearing and think about some of the items you use – any ideas? □

If you thought of weaving, then well done. Let's have a look at this way of making fabrics in a little more detail.

Weaving

Weaving is the most common way of making fabrics. Most weaving is still worked on looms. Lines of yarns (which are called the **warp**) are stretched down the loom while another yarn (called the **weft**) is passed over and under the warps from one side to the other.

Try making a cover for a book using weaving.
You will need some pins, some polystyrene tiles, some cotton fabric, an old paint brush, and some watered-down PVA glue.
Cut some 2 cm strips of fabric the length required to cover the book. Pin these to the top of the tiles, quite close together. These are your warp threads.
Using the other strips (these will be your wefts), weave the threads under and over the warps. Alternate each row as shown in the diagram.
Leave the ends free at the sides. Pin down these ends so that the weft strips are kept close together. Start each row with a new strip. Continue this until you have a piece of cloth large enough to make a book cover.
Paint the PVA glue all over the fabric and leave it to dry.
Remove the pins. You should now have a piece of fabric which can be made into a book cover. The weave of the fabric is called plain weave. □

Weaving a book cover can be fun but just imagine if you had to do this to make a much larger piece of fabric. Picking up every warp yarn as you did to make the book cover takes up a lot of time. On a commercial scale it would make the fabric very expensive. This is where the loom comes in as it weaves very quickly.

Loom

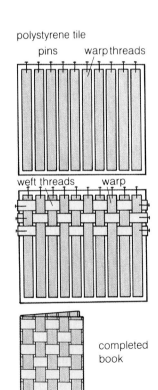

polystyrene tile
pins   warp threads

weft threads   warp

completed book

Weaving along!

Have a look at the following pictures of some different weaves.

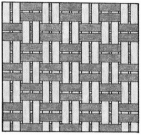
Hopsack

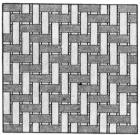
Twill

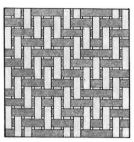
Herringbone

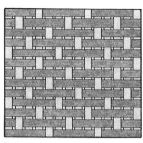
Sateen

See if you can make one or more of these different weaves out of strips of sugar paper. Can you explain how what you have done is different from plain weaving? □

Putting an edge on it

As the weft threads come down the outside edges of the warp threads a special kind of edge is made – a **selvedge** (the word comes from 'self edge'). These selvedges are special because they won't fray as the weft threads are wrapped around the side warp threads.

 Have a look at some fabrics and see if you can find a selvedge. □

Other weaves

You have probably seen towelling and velvet in the shops and at home. Both these fabrics are examples of a plain or twill weave with a **pile** inserted in the weaving. With the towelling the loops of the weave are left uncut, but with velvet they are cut to give a different finish.

Towelling

With towelling the extra surface area from the loops is very useful as it makes the fabric more absorbent. So when you are drying yourself with a cotton towel there is more of it to absorb the moisture from your body.

 Next time you have a shower or a bath try drying one of your legs with a cotton towel and the other leg with a cotton sheet. Which fabric dries your leg the best? □

Velvet

What about knitting?

Knitting is another way of making fabric. It can be done by hand
or machine. Knitting can be thick and chunky or it can be very fine.
Knitting is used to make jumpers, socks, and stockings. All fabric
made by knitting is stretchy. The amount of stretch and the
direction in which the fabric stretches depends on the way in
which the threads are interlocked together. There are a number of
different ways of interlocking threads when knitting either by
hand or machine.

If you want to try your hand at knitting get a number of people to
make little squares or rectangles of knitting.
Then sew these together and make a patchwork blanket.
Decide what to do with the blanket.□

Knitting by hand is only one way. You can also use a knitting
machine at home or at school. There are many different types of
machine available to choose from. Knitting machines make items
much quicker than hand knitting and the finish is very even and
professional looking.

Knitting can be very simple or very complicated.

Knitting machine

Keeping in the warmth

Fabrics made by knitting tend to be warm because air is trapped between the stitches.

 Why does trapped air make a fabric warm (see Unit 2 p. 14)? □

The one big problem, though, is that knitted fabrics can go out of shape easily if you don't look after them carefully (see Unit 13).

 Can you think of any more uses for knitted fabrics? □

More ways of making fabrics from yarns

Here are just a few more ways of making fabric from yarns:

◀**Macramé**, where knots are tied in yarns to make the fabric.

▲
Lacemaking, where bobbins are used to twist and knot the yarns together.

◀**Crochet**, where a hook is used to loop the yarn on itself.

Making fabric without a yarn

There are other ways of making fabric without using yarn, in other words by using the fibres as they are without spinning them into yarn first.

Felt is a very useful fabric which is made straight from fibres. Felt is used for making toys, hats, and carpets. It is very useful as it doesn't fray like weaving, or ladder like some knitting. However, it is not very strong so it might tear and pull apart and it doesn't wash well. It is easy to shape though, and it is a good insulator (keeps things warm).

Felt is used for toys, hats, and lining cutlery drawers.

Another fabric made straight from fibres is **bonded fibre fabric**. Disposable nappies, hospital gowns and masks, disposable dish cloths, and some interfacings are all made from this kind of fabric. With bonded fibre fabrics the fibres are glued together. Other examples of fabrics made straight from fibres are carpets, wall coverings, carpet tiles, blankets, padding, and insulation.

 Have a look at the clothes which you are wearing.
List the clothes which are made from weaving. Can you name the weaves?
List the clothes made from knitting. Can you name the methods used in the knitting?
List the other clothes and beside each one say how you think the fabric used to make it has been made. □

 Go into a room at home and list fifteen textile items that you can see in the room. For each item you name, say how you think the fabric used to make that item was made. □

Thinking, planning, and doing

Throughout this book you will be asked to do quite a few tasks.
These will help you to understand and to use the work covered in
each unit. All these tasks need quite a bit of thought if you are to
get the most out of them. After you have done the task it's a good
idea to think about how well you have done. In this way you can
work out how to do things better should you try a similar task at a
later stage. It may be that you think things could not be improved,
in which case well done!

Although there are as many ways of solving problems as there are
people in the world, it does help to have a plan. If you use a plan
you can make sure that you have thought of everything and
haven't left anything out.

You can use the following 'Step-by-Step' method for planning
textile tasks if you like. If you can come up with a method of your
own which works for you, then stick with it.

The Step-by-Step method for textiles

1 What have I been asked to do?

2 What are the important things to think about?

3 What ideas do I have?

4 What shall I choose to do?

5 Does my choice fit in with what I was
   asked to do?

6 How shall I set about the task?

7 Now I can get going!

8 How well did I do?

Now, let's take each of these steps and look at them in a little more
detail:

1 What have I been asked to do?
The first thing to make sure of is that you understand exactly what
it is you have been asked to do. If in doubt – *ask!*

2 What are the important things to think about?
Next, list the points that you need to think about when deciding
what to do. For example, you might think that some, or all, of the
following are important:
   what the item is to be used for;
   who will use the item;

the time you have to complete the task;
the expertise (skill) you might need;
any help you might need;
what equipment you will need and what is available;
what other people like or dislike;
how much money you have to spend.

3 What ideas do I have?

Having sorted out the things to think about, record any ideas that come to mind. It doesn't matter, at this stage, how daft these ideas may seem to be.

4 What shall I choose to do?

With all your ideas of possible things to do, take some time to make your final choice. You may want to test some of your ideas out first – on other people, on fabrics, on paper, etc. Check back to the points you made under 'things to think about' to help you.

5 Does my choice fit in with what I was asked to do?

Always make a point of checking your final choice to see if it fits and answers the task you are doing. It often helps if you ask someone else to check your idea with you.

6 How shall I set about the task?

You now need a plan. It's a good idea to make a plan of action to help you do the task. It will help you get things in order and give you something to follow so you don't miss out any important points. It's useful to make a list of the equipment and materials you need too.

DESIGN AND MAKE A SIMPLE TOY

1. Make a pattern.
2. Cut out fabric – felt and fur.
3. Make up ears.
4. Attach ears to front head in position.
5. Attach eyes and nose in place.
6. Join head back to head front along side and upper seams.
7. Make up four paws.
8. Attach to front body in position.
9. Join front body to back body leaving a gap for stuffing.
10. Join head to body.
11. Stuff toy – sew up hole.

7 Now I can get going!

Once you have got your plan of action, the equipment, and all the materials needed to answer the task, you can then get going.

8 How well did I do?

When you have finished, have a look at the way you worked. Think about the time it took you to finish the task and what the result was like. Would you change anything if you did the same task again?

Some things for you to do

Using the Step-by-Step method, make a collage based on the theme of transport. Use as many different fabrics as you can. □

Use the Step-by-Step method to make an item using one of the ways of making fabrics mentioned in this unit. The item could be:
  something to use
  something decorative
  something to play with. □

Here are some ideas to help you to decide:

Another look at this unit

1 Ways of making a fabric from yarns include:
   weaving – the interlacing of warp and weft threads;
   knitting;
   macramé;
   lacemaking;
   crochet.
2 Ways of making a fabric without having to use a yarn include:
   felting – wool or 50% wool blends where the fibres matt together;
   bonded fibre fabrics, e.g. disposable goods, where the fibres are glued together.
3 The fibres used to make these fabrics and the way they are put together give the fabrics different properties. It also gives us a wide variety of fabrics to choose from.
4 When you are given a task to do in textiles, try using the Step-by-Step method to help you. Think carefully about what you have been asked to do and what you need to consider; know the reasons for your choice; plan how you are going to tackle the task; and judge yourself and how you worked at the end.

UNIT 5
Colouring fabrics

Is colour important to you?

Colour is a very important thing. Most people notice the colour of something straight away – the colour of a car, jacket, room, furniture, etc. Also, most people have very strong likes and dislikes where colour is concerned. Colour is also used to describe certain feelings that people might have – green with envy, white with fright, red with anger, blue with cold, and so on.

How colours come about

All colours come from three primary (first) colours: red, yellow, and blue. These three colours cannot be made from other colours which is why they come first and are called primary colours. If you take any two primary colours and mix them together in equal amounts you will get secondary colours: green, orange, and violet.

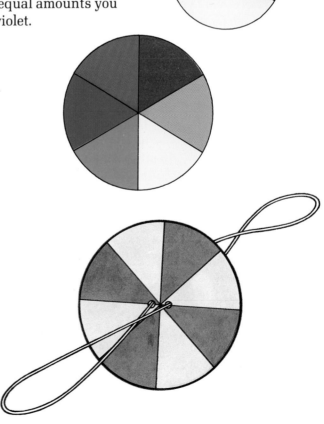

red + blue = violet
blue + yellow = green
yellow + red = orange

Try making a 'whizza' to see how colours come about.
Cut a circle of white cardboard about 4–6 cm in diameter.
Divide the circle into eight equal sections. Mark these sections with a pencil.
Choose one of the primary colours and colour every other section with that colour.
Choose another primary colour and colour in the missing sections.

Make two holes as shown in the picture of the whizza and thread about 1.50 m of string through the two holes.
Twist the string and twirl the whizza around. You should now see a secondary colour before your very eyes!
You can colour the other side with different primary colours to get another secondary colour.□

Even more colours

By mixing the primary and secondary colours, you can get lots of different tertiary (third-type) colours, for example:

    violet + red = burgundy
    red + orange = tan

Each colour on the colour wheel has a contrast colour – the colour *exactly* opposite it. So the contrast colour of red is green.

 Look at the colour wheel. What are the contrast colours of:
    yellow?
    blue? □

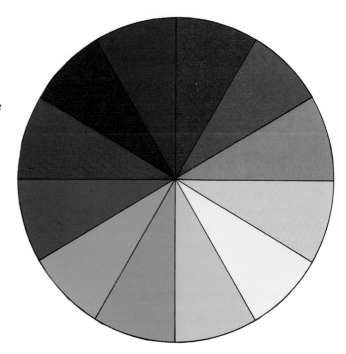

 Seeing red? What colour do you see?
Draw a 1 cm square on a piece of white paper.
Colour the square solid red.
Put a plain piece of paper beside the piece with the red square on.
Stare at the red square for two minutes (get someone to time you).
At the end of the two minutes, look straight away at the blank piece of paper. What colour do you see?
If you saw green for a split second, then this is what you would expect to see, as green is the contrast colour of red.
Try the same thing with other colours if you wish.
Can you find out why your eyes work in this way? □

If you mix different amounts of the primary colours together and add black or white as well, then all the other colours can be made.

You may have heard people talk about tints and shades. Do you know what these words mean?

A **tint** is any colour with white added to it.

A **shade** is any colour with black added to it.

A tint of blue

A shade of blue

 Have a go at making some colours. Try this using paint and see if you can find out how grey is made.
What colour is made from mixing all three primary colours? □

Colours can also be described as hot or cold. Reds and oranges are hot colours. Blues and greens are cold colours.

Getting the colour into fabric

When a fabric has been made from yarns (Unit 3) which, in turn, are made from fibres (Unit 2) it has to be 'finished' before it can be coloured. This is because the fabric is dull and dirty. It may also be stiff and have a funny shape. So all fabrics are finished in some way. These 'finishes' make the fabric look better; they make it feel nicer; and they help it to last longer and wear better.

Once the fabric has been bleached (to make it white) and washed (to get all the grease and dirt out) then it can be coloured or dyed. Nowadays dyeing is a very scientific business using a variety of chemicals. But it wasn't always like this.

Squashed beetles!

In Roman times crushed beetles were used to give a pink (cochineal) colour. Up until the 1800s all dyes came from plant and animal sources such as roots, leaves, berries, fish, and animals. In 1856 the first man-made dye was made from coal tar. This dye was 'fast' which meant that it did not come out of the fabric and was not affected in any way when the fabric was washed, rubbed, or put in direct sunlight.

We have come quite a long way since those Roman times. We also know a lot more about what gives a good result. If dyeing is to be done well then the colour must go right into, or penetrate, the fibres evenly. The dye should also be as colourfast as possible. The colour should not bleed, or run. The colour should not be affected by perspiration, washing, sunlight, fumes, sea water, or cleaning agents. It should not rub off on to the wearer. Just imagine wearing a pair of red shorts and being thrown into a swimming pool. How would you feel if, when you got out, you had red dye trickling down your legs! This actually happened to someone, so beware!

It is not always the *fabric* that is dyed though. Sometimes it is the fibres that are dyed before they are made into fabrics. Wool is often dyed in this way and gives a very even colour when it is made into fabric. Yarns can also be dyed first. Cotton gingham is made in this way. By dyeing the yarn first the check pattern can be made.

Cotton gingham

Usually, though, fabric dyeing is the cheapest way of dyeing. It also means that undyed (grey) cloth can be stored until the fashion colour has been decided. There are even times when whole items and garments are dyed.

Dyeing your own fabrics

Most fabrics are dyed commercially at some stage in the manufacturing process. But fabric and yarn can also be dyed at home or school, using either ready-made dyes or natural dyes.

There are many different types of dyes available today. There are also many ways of dyeing. It is important though to make sure that the dye you are going to use is suitable for the fibre content of the fabric to be dyed.

There are just a few points to think about before dyeing fabric.

1. What is the fabric made from?
   If natural fibres or viscose rayon are present then the fabric should dye well, as these fibres are absorbent. Synthetic fibres can be dyed but they don't dye as well as natural fibres because they don't absorb the dye so easily.
2. What is the original colour of the fabric?
   Have another look at the colour wheel. Check the colours that are produced by combining different colours. It may not come out as you expected – you have been warned!
3. How much time and what sort of equipment do you need?

The original colour of the fabric affects the finished result.

Have a go at the following to dye fabric using natural dyes:

You will need: a large enamel or stainless steel or ovenproof container; a rod or stick for stirring; some scales; a measuring jug; protective clothing; and loads of newspaper to cover the work surfaces.

Find some fabric to dye (try cotton, viscose, and polyester to see how they react). You will need about a metre.

Next decide on your natural dye – onion skins, beetroot, red cabbage, elderberries, nettles (if you can bear it), and carrot peelings are all easy to find. You will need about 300–500 g of one of these and 2 litres of water.

Finally, you will also need some **mordant** which will fix the dye in the fabric. This can be bought from most chemists and 15 g of alum or iron will be enough. Alum brightens the dye and iron darkens it. □

Getting down to dyeing!

1 **Preparing the dye solution**
   Put the source of your dye in the water. Cut up the plant in the water so you don't lose any of the colour. Boil the mixture for $\frac{1}{2}$–1 hour until you get a nice colour.
2 Take the mixture off the heat and strain the liquid into another pan.
3 **Preparing the fabric**
   Wet the fabric so that it will take the dye better by absorbing the coloured water more evenly. This will also remove any finish which can stop the dye from being taken up and from being fast.
4 **Dyeing**
   Put the wet fabric in the dye and stir well until the fabric is warm.
5 Dissolve the mordant in a little water and add this to the dye. Stir well.
6 If you can, leave the fabric in the dye for at least 10–12 hours. It can be left for up to 48 hours.
   Rinse the fabric thoroughly (this takes a long time).
   Dry the fabric.

Look at the different colours that have resulted from the use of different fabrics made from different fibres.

You could now make your fabric into an item, e.g. a cushion cover, shorts, or scarf. □

Using commercial dyes

If you are going to use commercial dyes such as Dylon at home or at school, do read the instructions carefully and then follow them exactly to get the best results. There are two types of dye that you can buy: hot water dyes and cold water dyes. Both types come in a wide variety of colours.

How to resist dyeing!

You can get some interesting effects by not letting the dye get to certain parts of the fabric. This is known as 'resist dyeing'. This means that certain parts of the fabric are not coloured. When the fabric is dry the result is two different colours. This can be repeated to put other colours into the fabric. The methods you can use to do this are **tie and dye** and **batik**.

Tie and dye

This is a very old way of dyeing which started in the Far East. The dye is stopped from getting to parts of the fabric by knotting, folding, clipping, tying, or binding the cloth. All kinds of string will prevent the dye penetrating, but nylon string is the most resistant to cold-water dyes. You can also use various objects to give interesting and unusual patterns, e.g. paper clips, clothes pegs, rubber bands, and even dental floss!

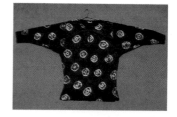

The important thing to remember is that all string, thread, or cord must be tied very, very tightly and knotted firmly so that it doesn't loosen when it is dyed. You can then dye with either natural or commercial dyes.

Batik

This is also called 'wax writing' because the wax which is 'painted' on to the fabric is used to prevent the dye from getting to the fabric. The waxed fabric keeps its original colour when the fabric is dyed. When the wax is removed the contrast between the dyed and undyed areas will give you a pattern.

Batik wax and cold-water dyes are easy to buy (from craft shops and suppliers). A cold-water dye must be used, otherwise the heat in the dye bath will melt the wax, which would undo all your hard work!

Dyeing is the name of the game!

Using the Step-by-Step method on p. 26, make an item for your home or your room using the 'resist' method of dyeing as described in this unit.☐

Here are some ideas to help you:

Another look at this unit

1 Colour is all around us. It is probably one of the first things we notice about something.
2 All colours are based on the primary colours: red, yellow, and blue, plus black and white.
3 Each primary, secondary, and tertiary colour has a contrast colour.
4 There are many different methods of dyeing due to the different fibres that are used to make fabrics. The fibre content and colour of the fabric must be taken into account.
5 A good dye is fast to bleeding, perspiration, washing, light, fumes, sea water, and cleaning agents. The colour should not rub off on to you either.
6 Some methods of 'resist dyeing' are tie and dye and batik.

UNIT 6

Getting print on to fabrics

Colouring by printing

Fabrics can be coloured by printing. Colours are put on to the fabric in a certain kind of pattern. There are several ways of colouring fabric by printing. The simplest way is hand block printing.

Hand block printing

This is the oldest way of printing designs on to fabric. But it is a slow method and therefore expensive. It is still used though to make expensive items such as silk scarves. The basic idea is that the design is traced on to a hard block of wood and the rest of the block is then cut away to leave the design behind. The dye is put on the pattern and the block is stamped on to the fabric. For every colour in the pattern a separate block must be used and great care must be taken to keep the design evenly spread over the fabric.

Fabric printing machine

 First, have a go at using potatoes to make some wrapping paper. You will need: a knife, some potatoes, some good quality absorbent dull paper, any paint that will stay on this paper, a paintbrush, water, protective clothing, and loads of newspaper.

Put layers of newspaper over the working surfaces. Make up the paint. Cut a potato in half using a sawing action to get a good smooth surface as this is the side with which you will be printing.

Then shape the potato to the design you want. The simpler the shape the more effective it is likely to be. Cover your block with paint using a paintbrush. Try out your design on a test piece of paper first. Now, print your design keeping the prints evenly spaced. Clear up and leave to dry. □

Going one step further

If you did the potato test you might like to try out some further ideas:
Try using different potato blocks and colours to make more complicated designs.
Try using different fruits and vegetables – some can be carved first, others just painted – or paint leaves, but make sure they are dried after cutting as they are sometimes wet. Scraps of wood, sponge, and leather can also be used as printing blocks.
Try printing fabrics using fabric paste dyes. They can be made into table mats, napkins/serviettes, bags, headscarves, and tablecloths.

When printing fabric be sure to wash the fabric first so that any finish is removed (see Unit 5 p. 31 and Unit 7 p. 41).□

Stencilling

Stencilling on paper and fabric is a good way to get quite professional results. You can make your own stencil from card and use it to print your own design. Or you can buy ready-made stencils from stationers and craft shops.

Try out some stencilling for yourself.
You will need:
some fabric which has been washed and ironed – try with cotton fabrics first;
some scrap fabric for a trial test;
some paper to put inside any double-sided item, such as a T-shirt, to stop the dye coming through;
some non-absorbent cardboard for the stencil;
a Stanley knife to cut out the design;
some masking tape, some dye paste in a saucer, and some scraps of synthetic sponge.

What to do

1 Draw your design onto the cardboard. Cut the design out very carefully with a Stanley knife. Be careful here because these knives are extremely sharp.

2 Take a piece of scrap fabric and tape the stencil onto it with short lengths of masking tape. Using the sponge, dip it into the saucer of dye paste, wiping it on the side of the saucer to get rid of any unwanted dye. Then, firmly and gently, press the sponge over the open section of the stencil. The harder you press, the stronger the colour. Remove the stencil and make sure the fabric dries thoroughly.

3 Repeat the second stage on your proper piece of fabric.

The fabric could then be used to make tablecloth motifs or perhaps an alphabet frieze for a child's room.□

Spraying it all about!

Another idea is to spray the dye over the stencil. This can be done quite easily with an old toothbrush and knife or a mouth-blown diffuser.

The toothbrush produces a splattered effect and the mouth-blown diffuser, because the dye paste has to be thinned down, gives very delicate patterns. Always follow the manufacturer's instructions with the mouth-blown diffuser to get the best results.

Using a mouth-blown diffuser

Screen printing

Screen printing is a more complicated method of printing but it still can be done at home or school.

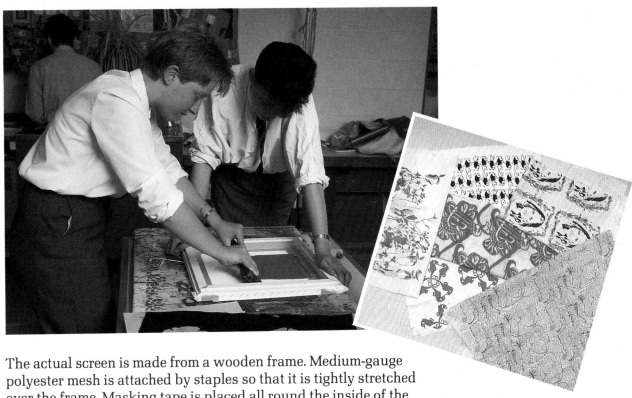

The actual screen is made from a wooden frame. Medium-gauge polyester mesh is attached by staples so that it is tightly stretched over the frame. Masking tape is placed all round the inside of the screen to stop any dye getting into unwanted places, and a stencil is placed between the screen and the fabric. A 'squeegee' is then used to cover the screen with dye. The stencil lets part of the dye through and so gives you a print.

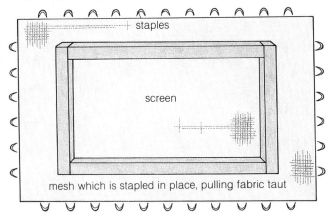

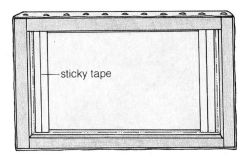

If you print on a table covered with newspaper and then polythene, this gives much better prints.

This is the simplest way of screen printing but there are other ways of putting a design on to a screen, e.g. by photography.

Screen printing on a larger scale

In industry screen printing is a popular way of printing fabric. It is costly though because a different screen has to be used for each colour in the design. Other methods used in industry to print fabrics include **flock**, **roller**, and **transfer** printing.

 Can you find out more about these methods? ■

You can try out transfer printing for yourself by using 'fabric crayons'. This is a quick and easy way of printing and is not very messy. You draw your design on to paper with the crayons. Then place your paper over some fabric and press down on the paper with a hot iron. The design is then transferred by the heat of the iron from the paper on to the fabric. The design will come out the other way round to how you have drawn it on the paper.

Something for you to do

 Using the Step-by-Step method, print a bought T-shirt or sweatshirt with a design or symbol that says something about what kind of person you are. For example, the design or symbol could show one or more of your interests or show something about your character. Other people should be able to guess that the shirt belongs to you just by looking at the design or symbol. ■

Another look at this unit

1 Fabrics can be printed to give them colour and design. If they are printed, the design is usually on one side, leaving the other side plain.
2 Block, stencilling, screen, and transfer are all ways of printing which can be done at home and school.
3 Block printing can be done with potatoes and other vegetables, fruits, leaves, scraps of wood, sponge, and leather.
4 Stencilling can give you professional results whether you make your own stencil or buy one.
5 Screen printing requires more equipment than the other methods but is well worth trying if you get a chance.
6 Transfer printing is quite easy if you use 'fabric crayons'.
7 Do try some, or all, of these methods of printing to make different fabrics look really something else!

UNIT 7

And now for the finishing touch!

Getting it finished

We now know how a fabric is made, coloured, and printed. In Unit 5 it was mentioned that fabrics are also 'finished'. We are now going to look at finishes in a little more detail to see why some fabrics are finished.

Making fabrics from fibres without using any finishes means that the fabrics keep any disadvantages that the fibres may have. For example, cotton fibres crease really easily, so if cotton fabric is not finished in some way it can be a bit of a pain to use and to look after. So, manufacturers use finishes on fabrics to make the fabric more useful to the consumer, i.e. you.

What do finishes do to fabric?

Finishes are used to make fabrics look nicer. They can also make fabrics more useful, for example, warmer, stiffer, longer lasting, or safer.

Let's look first at how fabrics can be made to look nicer. Some finishes, like **calendering**, give the fabric more shine. Cotton and linen are really dull-looking fabrics and so they are calendered to make them look nicer – although the finish is not permanent! **Beetling** does much the same for linen.

There are several ways in which fabrics can be made more useful. For example, cotton, viscose rayon, and polyamide fabrics are often brushed to give the fabric a furry surface. This makes it warmer to wear because air is trapped in the surface. Some fabrics need to be stiffened for certain jobs like being used for collars and cuffs. This is called **trubenizing**.

Then there are finishes which make the fabric last longer. Wool is moth-proofed to stop moths laying their larvae in the wool. The larvae eat the wool fibres and leave holes behind in the fabric. The chemicals which are used don't harm the wool but they smell really horrible to moths so they won't come anywhere near to lay their eggs.

Having a flaming good time!

Some finishes affect how the fabric will 'behave' when it is used. Flame-proofing is an example of this.

Different fabrics burn at different rates. Some fabrics give off a lot of smoke, and some smoke is really unpleasant. Knowing how a fabric behaves when you set light to it can be quite important. Indeed, it can be a matter of life and death!

 This is a good test to try on as many fabrics as you can. Wool, polyester, and cotton give the best results.
Cut 20 cm length strips of fabric, each about 3 cm wide. Attach each strip to a wire line as shown in the diagram.
It is important, for safety reasons, to attach one strip at a time and test it before attaching the next strip. Set each fabric alight and notice:

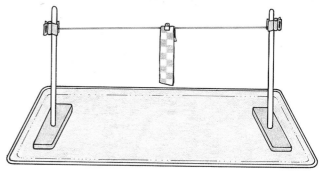

1 How the fabric reacts to the flame when the flame is held close to the fabric.
2 How quickly the fabric ignites (is set alight).
3 The time it takes to burn the entire strip of fabric.
4 What it smells like when it is burning.
5 The type and quantity of smoke produced.

Record your results in a table like this:

FABRIC	APPROACHING FLAME	IGNITION	TIME	SMELL	SMOKE	
Cotton						
Linen						
Wool						
Polyamide						

Why do you think it is important that children's nightwear doesn't burn easily?
What fabrics would you choose for children's nightwear?
What fabrics would you not use for children's nightwear? ▫

You probably found that cotton, linen, viscose rayon, and acetate all burn very easily and quickly. These fabrics can have a finish which makes them flame-proof but this can spoil their softness. Also, when they are washed in soap, a soap layer forms on the fabric which is flammable (will easily ignite). So it is important to wash these fabrics in soapless detergent.

Other ways of getting a finish

Other finishes are used to make the fabric wear better. A fabric which shrinks when washed is not much good. If it is a garment it can look downright silly!

 Try out some shrink tests for yourself.
Get some 10 cm squares of different fabrics containing a variety of fibres. Measure the squares exactly.
Wash the squares in very hot water with a lot of agitation (movement).
Dry the squares, measure again, and notice the difference.
Which squares have shrunk the most? ☐

Wool shrinks a lot unless it is treated carefully when washed (see Unit 13 p. 87). Remember the scales on wool that you saw under the microscope (Unit 2 p. 14)? These scales tangle and matt together when wool is washed badly. Wool can be made shrink-resistant by removing the scales during manufacture. It is then sold as 'machine-washable wool'. Or the wool fibres can be coated with nylon: this is called the 'Dylan' process.

PURE
NEW WOOL

MACHINE WASHABLE

Why are some fabrics pre-shrunk?

Some fabrics, like cottons and rayons, are pre-shrunk. This is because they can be stretched during weaving, so they often shrink when they are first washed. Sometimes the fabric is pre-shrunk before you buy it. But you can still get some shrinkage when you wash pre-shrunk fabric the first couple of times. Sometimes we can use this shrinking quality to our advantage, for example, when we shrink jeans to mould to our bodies.

Keeping water out

Some fabrics need to be water-repellent, e.g. coats and jackets.

 Get some 10 cm squares of wool, cotton, polyamide, and PVC.
Put a drop of water on the surface of each fabric and watch what happens.
Does it repel the water, i.e. does the water remain in its droplet form on the surface of the fabric?
Or is the fabric slightly absorbent because the droplet breaks down and is absorbed very slowly?
Or is the fabric very absorbent because the water is quickly taken up and absorbed by the fabric?
Some fabrics, e.g. PVC, are naturally water-repellent, while other fabrics only become so after they have been treated. ▪

What about cottons and rayons?

Cottons and rayons are very absorbent. Unless they are treated they are not suitable for outerwear. So these fabrics are coated with a finish which stops the fibres from absorbing anything. A close weave is also a lot more water-repellent than an open weave. Wool is also very absorbent but it does not feel wet until it has absorbed 40% of its weight in water!

Some fabrics, such as furnishing fabrics, need to be stain resistant. The fabric is treated so that it won't absorb liquids, in much the same way as a fabric is made water-repellent. You may have seen advertisements, posters, and labels for some carpets which have been treated in this way.

All creased up!

Some fabrics crease easily and the creases won't drop out. This can be a nuisance and it looks terrible. After all, most people don't want to look as if they have slept in their clothes!

 Find some 10 cm squares of cotton, viscose rayon, wool, and polyamide.
Simply screw up the fabric in your hand and hold it for 1 minute.
Open your hand and notice how creased the fabric is.
Repeat again, only this time hold it in your hand for 3 minutes.
What is the difference? Which fabric creased the most and which fabric creased the least?
Which fabric is the most crease resistant? ▢

Cotton, linen, and viscose rayon all crease badly. They can be treated not to crease, but this makes them a little stiffer. Also the finish is not always permanent after a lot of washing.

Permanently creased

Other fabrics need to have permanent pleats or creases put in them in certain places. The thermoplastic fibres – polyester, polyamide, and acrylics – can all be heat set and can be permanently pleated so they keep their creases very well even when washed many times over.

You should have discovered that linen, cotton, and rayon crease very easily but the creases do not last. So, finishes are applied to them which help them to keep their creases in place.

All the finishes used affect the way in which the fabric reacts when washed and dried. It is best to read the manufacturer's care label so you know the best way to treat a fabric.

Another look at this unit

1 Finishes are applied to fabrics by manufacturers to make fabrics more suitable for their chosen use.
2 Finishes can be applied to make the fabric look nicer, e.g. calendering, beetling, brushing, and trubenizing.
3 Finishes can be applied to make the fabric more useful, for example to make the fabric last longer, e.g. moth-proofing and flame-proofing; or to improve the wear of the fabric, e.g. shrink resistance, water-repellency, stain resistance, crease resistance, and permanent creasing.
4 These finishes often affect the way fabrics are handled, so make sure that you look at garment and item labels and treat them as the manufacturer suggests.

UNIT 8

One way to sew it up

Machine power!

At some time you will probably want to use a machine to get things done faster and better. Whatever machine you use, here are a few simple guidelines to help you. Remember to get the instruction book or manual that goes with the machine as it will help you a lot. There are many different types of sewing machine available today which is why a manual is helpful.

An idiot's guide to the sewing machine

Although sewing machines vary in price from those which are very basic to those which have loads of gadgets and extra bits and pieces, there are basic principles which govern the way all of them work.

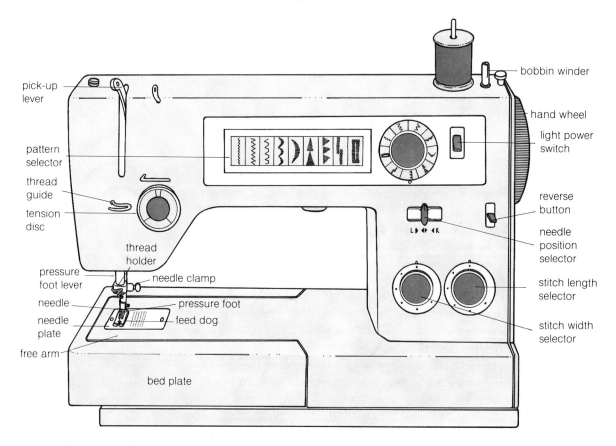

A closer look at the sewing machine

Let's take a look at some of the parts of a sewing machine.

Thread holder
This is where you put the thread when winding the bobbin and when stitching.

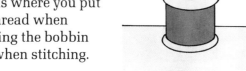

Hand wheel
This has direct contact with the needle. When you want to do exact stitching, turn the hand wheel towards you. Loosen the inner wheel when you want to wind the bobbin as this inactivates the needle.

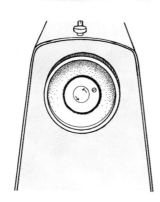

Stitch length selector
You can alter this depending on the length of stitch you want. See the chart on p. 51.

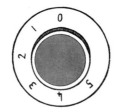

Pattern selector
You adjust this for the pattern you want.

Stitch width selector
You alter this according to the width of stitch you want. See the chart on p. 51.

Tension disc
For a machine stitch to be balanced (see p. 52) the top and bobbin tension must be even. You can alter the stitch tension by turning this disc.

Light power switch
This turns on a light on the machine. It is very useful as it saves you straining your eyes as you work.

Pick-up lever
This picks up the thread from the reel to get ready for the next stitch. When starting and finishing stitching, the pick-up lever should be at its highest point which is when it has picked up the thread.

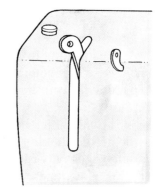

Needle clamp
You undo this to replace the needle.

Pressure foot
This holds the fabric in position when stitching.

Pressure foot lever
This is used to operate the pressure foot.

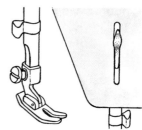

Bed plate
This is the flat bed where you place the fabric when machining.

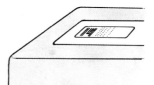

Feed dog
This is the small teeth found below the pressure foot that move the fabric through the machine while stitching.

A **free-arm machine** is one where the bed plate can be removed. This leaves the width of the bobbin case for machining. This is useful for machining round small areas such as sleeves.

Trying your hand at machining

 Get a sheet of lined paper and try machining along the lines. You don't need to thread the machine first.

Don't use a new needle as the paper will make it blunt.

Follow these simple rules:

1 Set the stitch length to 2½, the stitch width to 0, and the needle position to centre with the needle out of the bobbin case (in case the needle breaks). Switch on the machine.
2 Place the paper in from the front with most of it on the left of you.
3 Use the hand wheel to lower the needle into the paper at the place where you want to start stitching.
4 Lower the pressure foot.
5 Apply pressure to the foot control and, using both hands, guide the paper so that you can stitch on the line. Don't push or pull the paper with your hands; let the feed dog take it through at its own rate.
6 At the end, finish by leaving the pick-up lever at its highest point – the needle should be out of the paper. Lift the pressure foot and remove the paper towards the back of the machine.

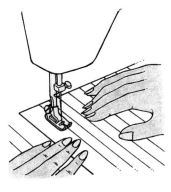

Try this a few times. To check your stitching is accurate, hold the paper up to the light and there should be a line of holes on the lines of the paper.

Now try the following:

1 Adjust the stitch length to 4 (make sure the needle is out of the bobbin case when you do this, otherwise it might break). Machine. The stitch is now longer.
2 Adjust the stitch length to 1. Machine. The stitches are now very small, like a perforated line.
3 Adjust the stitch length to 2½. Draw some curves on the paper like this:

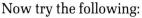

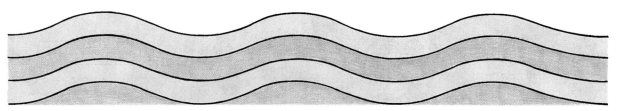

Machine slowly along the lines using both hands to guide the paper. As you get more confident, try tighter curves like these:■

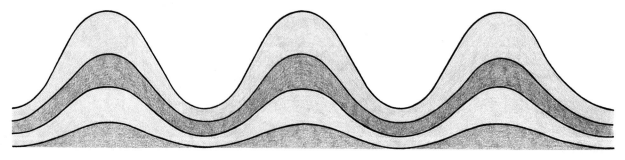

Going round corners

Draw some corners on a piece of paper and stitch along the lines, turning the corners like this:

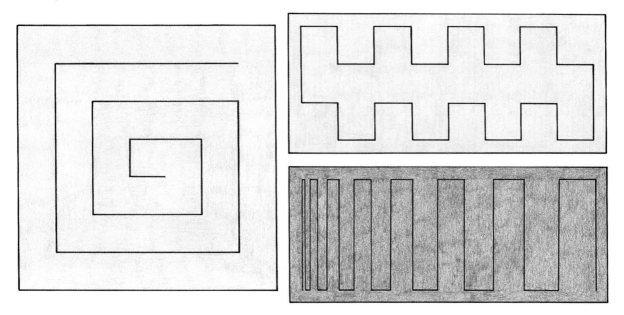

Start stitching as before. As you get near to a corner, stop machining and work the last few 'stitches' by turning the hand wheel. Leave the needle in the corner. Lift the pressure foot up and turn the paper round so that you can now stitch along the line. Lower the pressure foot and you are ready to go off again.

Here are some other patterns that you might like to try:

These are all good fun to do and good practice as well!■

And now for the real thing!

Having got so far, you are now ready to start machining on fabric. Before you start there are a few things to think about. You have to choose both machine needles and threads in relation to the weight and fibre content of the fabric you are stitching.

What machine needle should you use?

Here is a guide for machine needles:

Fabrics	Needle size	Needle type
Lightweight – cotton lawn, silk, lace	11 or 80 (metric size)	Sharp point
Medium weight – polycottons, cottons, e.g. needlecord, poplin, and prints	14 or 90	Sharp point
Heavyweight – woollens, cottons, e.g. corduroy, velvet, terry-towelling, gaberdines	16 or 100	Sharp point
All knitted fabrics	According to weight	Ball point

Threading your way along

It's very important that you use a thread which matches the fibre content of the fabric. In this way the fabric will stretch without puckering and can be cared for quite easily. Here are some examples of which thread to use with different fabrics:

Thread	Fabric
Gütermann	All fabrics
Drima	All fabrics – fibre content doesn't matter
Sylko 40	Lightweight naturals
Sylko 50	Medium and heavyweight naturals
Supreme	All synthetics

Getting your pedal to the metal!

Now we are really ready to get down to some machining.
1 Wind the bobbin according to the instructions in the machine's manual – remember to loosen the hand wheel.

2 Thread the machine, top and bottom, according to the machine's manual.

3 With the needle out of the needle hole of the throat plate (otherwise the needle will break in half), adjust the machine to the stitch width and needle position you want.

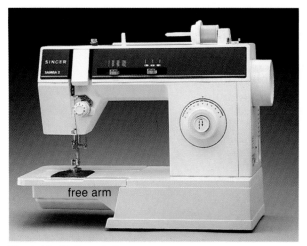

Straight stitch and zigzag

Semi-automatic

Automatic

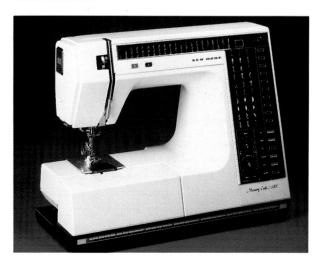

Computerized

Getting it stitched up

Here is a rough guide to help you work out what stitch length, stitch width, and needle position you need:

	Stitch length	Stitch width	Needle position
Straight stitch	$2\frac{1}{2}$	0	Centre
Gathering	4	0	Centre
Zig-zag	2	3-4	Centre

Testing it out

It's a good idea to test your machine stitching on a scrap of fabric.
Find a piece of fabric of the same type as you will be using. If you can
use a double piece of fabric this is an even better test, as you are more
likely to stitch two lots of fabric together than just one thickness.

If you get a loopy stitch then you will need to adjust the top tension.
If the tension is still not right then try the bobbin tension, but only as
a last resort as it is not easy to do.

The stitch is right when both the top thread and the bobbin thread
interlock between the two pieces of fabric. The stitch should hold
when pulled and should look the same on both sides.

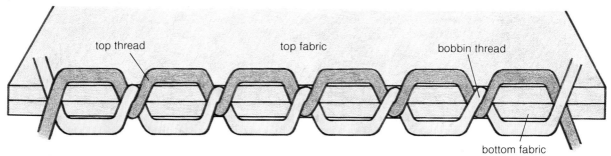

It will look like this if the top tension is too loose:

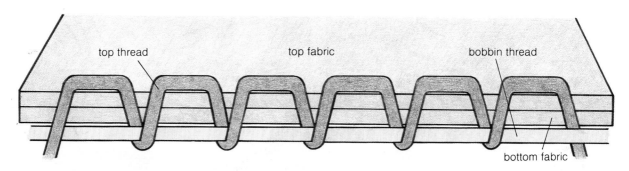

It will look like this if the top tension is too tight:

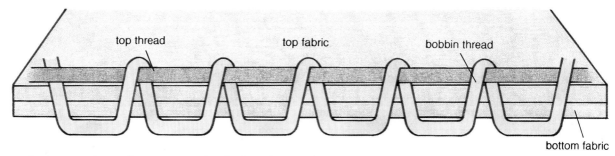

Before you adjust the tension, check that the machine is threaded
correctly. Often it is incorrect threading, rather than the tension,
which can be the cause of the problem.

Powering up the machine

Here are the basic steps to machining:
1 Put the threads towards the back of the machine. Make sure the needle and pressure foot are up.
2 Put the fabric between the feed dog and the pressure foot.
3 Lower the pressure foot.
4 Lower the needle with the hand wheel and push it right the way into the fabric.
5 Start machining.

Starting to machine

At the end

When you have finished:
1 Work the last few stitches by turning the hand wheel.
2 Check the needle is out of the fabric and that the pick-up lever is at its highest point.
3 Lift the pressure foot.
4 Pull the threads towards the back of the fabric (to stop the needle from breaking). Cut the threads, leaving long ends out of the machine and the fabric.
   You can fix the ends by:
   weaving them in and out of the last few stitches;
   knotting – make sure they are well tied;
   reversing the machine;
   or machining on the spot.
   Look up how to do these last two in your machine's manual.

If your stitching is not right, check in the manual to find out what is wrong. Any manual should tell you what to look for and what to do.

A task for you to do

Make a pencil case or book cover for yourself using the sewing machine. Decorate the item you make with some machine stitching in a pattern of your choice. Use the Step-by-Step method to help you. □

Another look at this unit

1 Using a sewing machine is quite straightforward as long as you follow a few basic rules.

2 Get to know the manual for any sewing machine you use – all your questions will be answered there!

3 Most machines have the same common parts which carry out the same functions.

4 Before using a machine on fabric for the first time, practise getting the feel of things by stitching (without thread) on paper.

5 Before machining fabric, make sure that you have the right type and size of needle, the right type of thread, and the right stitch length, stitch width, and needle position for the fabric you are using.

6 If things go wrong always check in the machine's manual first – it is usually something very simple and obvious!

UNIT 9

Adding an extra bit of something

Textile customizing

Fabrics, garments, and any textile item can be personalized by adding some decoration. Decoration makes the item more individual and easily identified as yours. There are many ways of doing this as you will see in this unit. You don't need a sewing machine for all the suggestions as some of the ideas can be worked by hand. Although some of the ideas will take some time to do, they are well worth the time and effort spent because your item will look very different from everyone else's.

Getting yourself organized

It's a good idea to have some equipment with you when you are working with textiles. Here are some ideas:

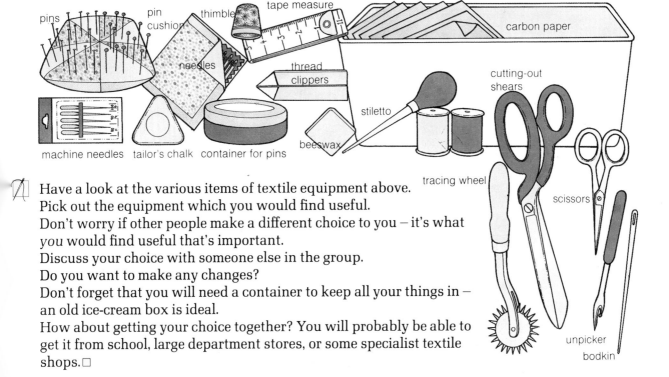

Have a look at the various items of textile equipment above.
Pick out the equipment which you would find useful.
Don't worry if other people make a different choice to you – it's what *you* would find useful that's important.
Discuss your choice with someone else in the group.
Do you want to make any changes?
Don't forget that you will need a container to keep all your things in – an old ice-cream box is ideal.
How about getting your choice together? You will probably be able to get it from school, large department stores, or some specialist textile shops.□

A word of caution

With all the techniques suggested in this unit it is a good idea to try out some of the ideas first before diving straight in. Suitable fabrics will be suggested at the beginning of each technique. Remember that threads should be suitable for the fabrics chosen. If you have any problems, have another quick look at Unit 8 p. 50.

Embroidery

Embroidery is probably the first thing that most people would think of in the way of fabric decoration.

There are several fabrics made specially for embroidery. If you are embroidering clothing, then the fabric should suit the garment (see Unit 12). Good fabrics for beginners include cotton calico, cotton gaberdine, and cotton poplin. Wool flannel is good too, but it is expensive.

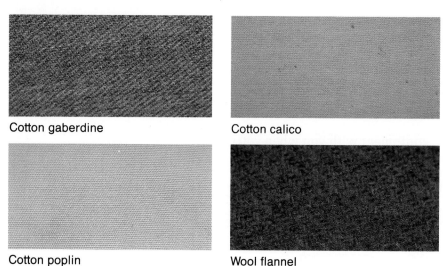

Cotton gaberdine

Cotton calico

Cotton poplin

Wool flannel

Threads

When it comes to threads for embroidery, there are again a number to choose from.

One type is called **stranded cotton**. This thread works well with most embroidery stitches and is a good choice for a beginner. It has six strands of thread loosely twisted together. These strands can be split up to suit your ideas.

Needles

A **crewel needle** is the best to use for most embroidery. This type of needle has a sharp point, is of medium length, and has a large eye for easy threading. The thread should be able to pass through the eye without chafing.

Frames

Frames can be bought from craft shops. Frames help to keep an even tension on the fabric and to avoid puckering. The most useful kind of frame for general use is a ring, hoop, or tambour. A tambour has an inner and an outer ring made from wood, metal, or plastic, with a screw for adjusting the tension of the fabric. Frames are available in a variety of sizes.

Tambour

Transferring the design

Draw your design on paper first and then use one of these methods:

1 The easiest way is to use dressmakers' carbon paper. Choose a colour which will show up on your fabric.

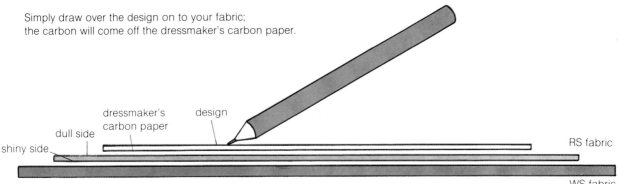

Simply draw over the design on to your fabric;
the carbon will come off the dressmaker's carbon paper.

shiny side

dull side

dressmaker's carbon paper

design

RS fabric

WS fabric

2 Or you can use 'tailor's chalk' to mark your design.
3 Yet another way is to mark the design on paper by making holes with a needle and then to sprinkle French chalk over the holes. The chalk goes through the holes on to the fabric.

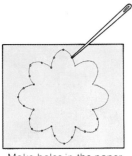
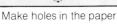

Make holes in the paper

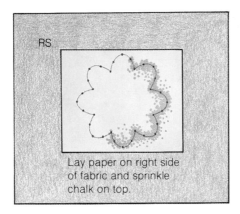

RS

Lay paper on right side of fabric and sprinkle chalk on top.

Remove paper and you have the design.

Ask your teacher for help when deciding what method to use or for what to do when you have decided which method you are going to use.

Stitches

There are many stitches you can use for embroidery. Here are some of the basic ones.

Running stitch

This is used for making outlines and creating simple line effects. Pass the needle over and under the fabric at regular intervals.

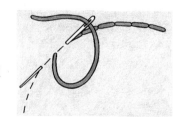

Backstitch

This is used for making outlines. Make a stitch backwards, bringing the needle out some way in front of the starting point. Then make another stitch backwards to meet the beginning of the last stitch, and so on.

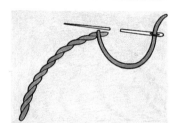

Stem stitch

This is used for outlines, lines, and fillings. The thread is kept on the same side of the needle all the time. Bring the needle out to the left, halfway along the previous stitch, and so on. The stitches should overlap each other.

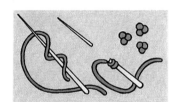

French knots

Bring the needle up at the place required, wrap the thread round the point of the needle once, and re-insert the needle. Hold the thread firmly with the thumb and pull the needle through smoothly and quickly.

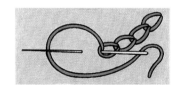

Chain stitch

This is used as an outline or filling stitch. Bring the needle through the fabric and insert it into the same hole. Bring the needle out on the same side of fabric a little farther forward. Wrap the thread round the needle. Pull the needle through the fabric. Repeat, forming a row of loops, with each loop securing the previous stitch.

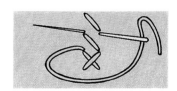

Cross stitch

Bring the needle up at the bottom right-hand corner, go down at the top left corner, coming out at the bottom left corner. Go down again at the top right-hand corner and so on to the next stitch.

Couching

This is used to outline a design or as a filling. Lay a thread on the fabric and tie it down with tiny stitches made at regular intervals along its length.

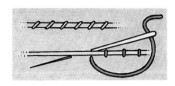

Satin stitch

This is used for fillings. It is best worked on a frame. The stitches can be of varying lengths but must lie flat and even.

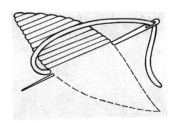

All these stitches are the basic ones and there are many variations based on them. If you want to find out more have a look in an embroidery book.

How about having a go at using some of these embroidery techniques? Your theme is 'cover-up'. Using the Step-by-Step approach, interpret this in any way you like, using embroidery techniques to make a personalized item.
See if you can invent any new stitches.□

Doing it for 'free'!

Some very unusual and effective results can be produced using free machine embroidery. No, it doesn't mean that you don't have to pay! Try this for yourself and see how you get on. Use a cotton fabric to try it out on.

1 Keep the fabric taut in a frame. Place the frame so that the right side of the fabric is on the inside of the hoop.
2 A single needle is used and most threads are suitable, although you can buy special machine embroidery threads.
3 Remove the pressure foot and drop the feed dog. Set the machine to straight stitch.
4 Machine steadily, moving the fabric under the needle to create a design. You might like to try to write your name, or to work some curls and loops. It's like drawing with the machine.

Whip stitch is an effect created by the bobbin thread looping over the top thread, just as if the stitch is not balanced properly. This is how you do 'whipping':

1 Place the fabric in a frame as before.
2 Thread the top with polyester thread and use machine embroidery thread for the bobbin.
3 Tighten the top tension (or loosen the bobbin tension if that doesn't work).
4 Set the machine to straight stitch. Drop the feed dog and remove the pressure foot.
5 Machine steadily and the loops should just appear.

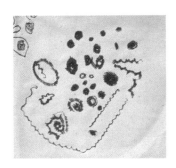

Automatic patterns

Some machines do embroidery patterns automatically when they are specially set up. Here are some of these patterns:

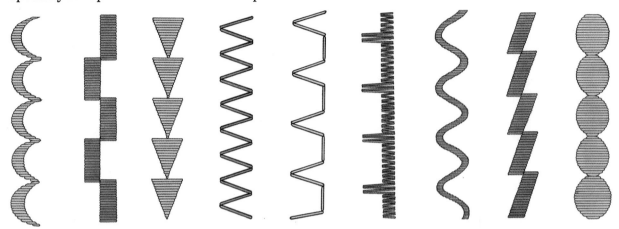

Follow the machine's manual. If you can use a machine with a microchip in it, then you will find many more patterns to play with!

Appliqué work

Appliqué means applying one fabric on top of another. Firmly woven cotton is a good choice of fabric for appliqué work. Both fabrics should be of the same fibre content as they will be washed and ironed together. Appliqué shapes seem to work best if they are kept simple.

 Now try your hand (and machine) at this:

First using the sewing machine:

Use one piece of fabric for the background and cut a simple shape from another piece of fabric. If you can use two different colours the design will stand out more. Make sure that the straight of the grains (see Unit 11) go the same way.

1 Tack the shape in place on the background fabric.
2 Machine (through both pieces of fabric) round the fabric you want to appliqué (stitch length $2\frac{1}{2}$; stitch width 0).
3 Carefully trim appliqué fabric back to the stitching.
4 Set the machine to satin stitch (stitch length $\frac{1}{4} - \frac{3}{4}$; stitch width 2–3). Stitch round the shape making sure the raw edge is covered.

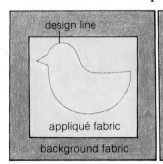

design line

appliqué fabric

background fabric

machine stitching

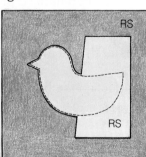

RS

RS

Machine carefully over trimmed edge.

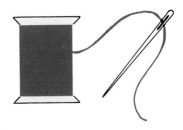

Now by hand:

1 Draw your design on paper and cut it out.
2 Pin on to the appliqué fabric. Try to match the straight of the grain on the appliqué fabric to that of the background fabric. Cut round the shape leaving about 1 cm of fabric outside it for turnings. Remove the pattern from the fabric.
3 Cut out the appliqué shape in lightweight interfacing to the exact size you want it to be.
4 Place the interfacing on the wrong side of the appliqué fabric. Turn the surplus fabric to the interfacing side and tack:

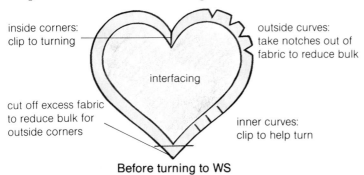

inside corners: clip to turning

outside curves: take notches out of fabric to reduce bulk

interfacing

cut off excess fabric to reduce bulk for outside corners

inner curves: clip to help turn

Before turning to WS

Turned to the WS of appliqué patch

5 Now place the appliqué patch on to the right side of the fabric and tack. If you don't want to see where the patch has been sewn on, then oversew it in place. If you are using embroidery thread, then use an embroidery stitch to stitch it in place. Some of the stitches which can be used are shown opposite.
  Can you think of any more stitches you could use?
6 Press the finished result. Remember to use a setting on the iron which is suitable for the type of fabric you are using (see Unit 13 p. 86). □

running stitch

cross stitch

blanket stitch

chain stitch

Quilting

This is where two fabrics are sewn together with something soft in between them. The fabrics for quilting are divided into those fabrics you can use for the top of the quilt and those fabrics used for the bottom.

The top layer of quilting can be plain or patterned. It should be smooth and of light- to medium-weight fabric. Cotton poplin, cotton calico, and any polycotton print are good choices for anyone starting out. The bottom layer can be the same as the top, or else any fabric that is cheap, and requires the same type of care as the top fabric, can be used.

The most common filling to use is polyester wadding. This can be bought from most fabric shops in various weights. It is washable, lightweight, warm, and easy to work with.

The threads you use for quilting must be strong – start with a mercerized cotton thread (size 40 or 50).

A quilting we go!

Assemble the fabrics as follows:

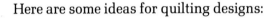

top layer

wadding

bottom layer or lining

Tack from the centre of the fabric to the outside at each corner, and in between if necessary. Be sure that all fabrics are flat.

Now you are ready to start quilting. There are many ways of doing this.

Quilting by hand

Simply work running stitches over the designs. Make sure that the ends are well secured. Remove the tacking stitches and press.

Here are some ideas for quilting designs:

Quilting by machine

1 With tailors' chalk and a ruler, draw a line across the fabric. Thread the machine, using appropriate thread and needles for the fabric. Attach a quilting pressure foot to the machine. Set the machine to stitch-length 3, stitch-width 0, and needle position centre. Test on a piece of scrap fabric and wadding, then stitch along the line.

2 Now, get the 'quilter' (or attach it if it is separate) – this is part of the quilting pressure foot. Line this up with your row of stitching and move the needle over until you have the width you want for your second row of stitching. Tighten the screw on the quilter. This will make sure that you stitch in straight rows.

3 Machine the second row of stitching, keeping the quilter on the first row all the time. Repeat this for the third row, with the quilter on the second row, and so on until you have covered the fabric. Try to keep the bulk of the fabric to your left while you are working.

4 For the rows going in the other direction: first mark a line in tailors' chalk, stitch along it, and then repeat steps **2** and **3**.

Free quilting

For this, set the machine up in the same way as for machine embroidery (see p. 59). Put your fabric in a hoop or frame, take the pressure foot off, and put the feed dog down. Machine steadily, making your own designs.

 Make a piece of soft sculpture (a three-dimensional item modelled in fabric) using some or all of the techniques described in this unit. The theme that you use and the item that you make is up to you. Why not take 'food' as a theme? Don't forget the Step-by-Step approach!□

Another look at this unit

1 All forms of hand decorative work help to make a textile item personalized and individual.

2 Designs can be transferred by dressmakers' carbon paper and/or tailors' chalk.

3 Always experiment with cotton fabric, e.g. cotton poplin or cotton calico. If a technique is new to you this will give you better results and more confidence to try further ideas.

4 Always practise on a scrap piece of fabric before doing the real thing.

5 Choose machine needles and threads suitable for the fabrics you are using. Machine embroidery thread can be used on most fabrics and is available in a variety of colours.

6 If you want to mix fabrics together, choose those which need the same kind of care (i.e. washing and ironing).

7 Above all, feel free to experiment and test out your own ideas and designs. Only in this way will you be able to turn an item into one that is exclusively *yours!*

UNIT 10
The clothes on your back

Why do we wear clothes?

What a daft question you might think. We wear clothes to keep us warm and because in most parts of the world it is not acceptable to go around naked. But is it as simple as this?

 Have a good look at these pictures. Write down why you think the people shown are wearing these particular clothes:

Some things to think about are:
- the job that they are doing
- the amount of money they might want to spend
- the climate in which they live
- the attitudes of people around them, e.g. conventional or modern attitudes
- their religious beliefs
- the dangers they are likely to face
- the type of occasion it is
- whether or not they could make the clothes themselves
- what they want to wear or feel comfortable in
- the self-image they have or wish to portray. □

So there are many reasons why people wear clothes. Sometimes we have to wear certain types of clothes, e.g. protective clothes or a uniform, like the one some people have to wear to school.

How uniform is your uniform?

 Make a rough sketch of your ideal school uniform.

Remember that people come in different shapes and sizes. Also think about some of the things you do at school which mean that you need practical clothing.

Do you think it is possible to please everyone?

Compare your sketch with the sketches of three or four other people in the class. How many similarities are there?

Do you think school uniform is a good or a bad thing to have? Discuss this in your group. Make a list of all the points for and against school uniform. □

What's your size?

Before buying clothes, or a pattern and fabric (see Unit 11), it's a good idea to know your measurements. It is worth knowing them just in case you can't try on clothes in the shop.

Here are some useful tips for taking measurements:

1 Use a reliable tape measure – not one that has been stretched.
2 Try to get a friend to measure you – it is much easier than trying by yourself. Ask your friend to stand to one side of you so they can see the tape measure almost all the way round you. Also this means that you can't cheat on the measurements!
3 Don't wear too many layers or else the measurements will be false.
4 Have the tape measure resting smoothly on your body, not pulled so tightly you can't breathe. Patterns and clothes allow some extra in their measurements so there is no need to add any extra of your own.

What to measure

The basic measurements you will need for most clothes are the bust/chest, waist, and hips. Other measurements might also be useful. Here is a list and a couple of diagrams so you can see where the numbered parts are:

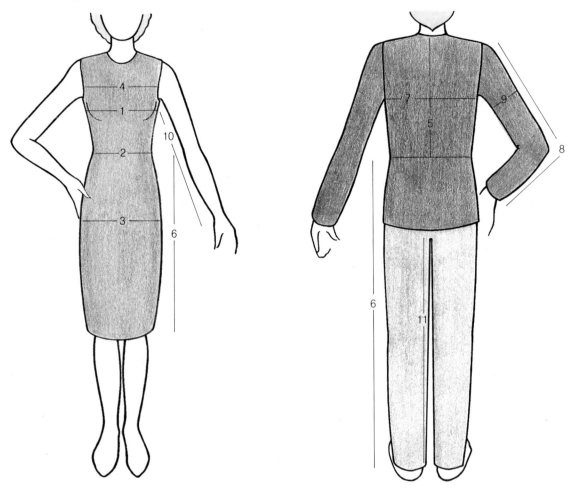

1 Bust/chest – measure round the fullest part.
2 Waist – measure round the natural waistline.
3 Hips – measure round the fullest part (not round the hipbones).
4 Chest width.
5 Nape – from the bone at the bottom of your neck down your back to your waist.
6 Waist to finished length (of skirt or trousers).
7 Back width.
8 Outside arm – measure with the elbow bent, otherwise your sleeves will be too short!
9 Round arm.
10 Inside arm.
11 Inside leg.
12 Crotch length – for trousers and shorts. To measure this sit on a hard chair and measure from the chair to the back of your waist.

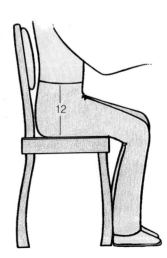

Buying clothes

It is best to buy nightwear, shirts, blouses, dresses, jackets and coats according to your bust/chest size. Buy trousers, skirts, and shorts according to your waist or hip size.

 Get a friend to help you take your measurements. □

What you wear says a lot about you as a person. Some people like to wear clothes that make them look attractive, while for other people comfort is far more important. Whatever you think is important, it is a good idea to think about your body shape and colouring when buying clothes, as well as your good and not so good points. Here are some guidelines to help you.

Body shape

1 Using line to help you: lines going up and down fabric give the impression of height and slimness. Lines going across the fabric tend to make people look shorter and wider.
2 Using colour to help you: dark colours make people appear slimmer and light colours have the opposite effect. Warm colours, e.g. reds, yellows, and oranges, make people seem larger. Cool colours of the same intensity as the warm colours have a slimming effect. Very bright colours make the figure appear larger than if the same, but subdued, colours are used.
3 Using pattern and texture to help you: a small print on a large figure or a large print on a small figure can look unbalanced. Fluffy, bulky, and heavily-textured clothes make people look wider.

By using accessories such as belts, badges, brooches, and necklaces, you can emphasize your good points by drawing the eye to them. If you have a large chest or bust, avoid wearing clothes that are tight across this area and have fussy necklines. If you have a small chest or bust, then you will look good wearing shirts or blouses which have gathers, pockets, or tucks in them. Tight-fitting clothes are fine if you have a slim figure. But clothes that are far too tight if you are large only make this more obvious.

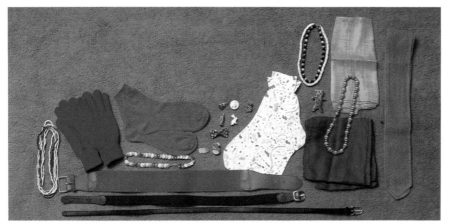

Colouring

Colour can also be a problem for some people. Generally speaking, fair-haired, fair-skinned people can wear most colours. People with dark skin look good in bright, clear colours, such as red, blue, and bright green. People who have a rosy complexion can soften it by neutral or cool colours such as grey, dark green, or blue. They should try to avoid 'hot' colours as these will emphasize a rosy complexion.

Looking good

Do remember that these are only guidelines, so don't stick to them rigidly. What you like and dislike, plus what you feel comfortable and confident wearing, are all very important. Fashion has a large part to play in what some people buy. But be aware that ultra-trendy and up-to-date clothes will date very quickly. If you don't wear them very much then they will not work out to be such a good buy as clothes which don't date so quickly. Also, different personalities and age groups often like different clothes. With a wide range of clothes to choose from today most people's tastes can be catered for.

When buying clothes think about how much you can afford to spend and try not to exceed this amount too much. Think about the occasion or occasions when you may want to wear the item. Also think about what else you have got to wear with the item. Don't forget, either, to look to see how the item should be cared for – can you wash it at home or does it have to be dry cleaned? Check the item as well – how has it been made, are the buttonholes well finished, are there any flaws in the fabric?

You can buy clothes from many places: department stores, boutiques, mail-order catalogues, specialist shops, and markets, to name but a few. They all have their advantages and disadvantages, so think carefully before parting with any money. Remember to keep the receipt in case you have to return the item to the shop for any reason. Also keep any care labels and follow them carefully to keep your clothes in a good condition (see Unit 13).

 Where do you go to buy your clothes?
In small groups, discuss your reasons for buying your clothes where you do. □

What to wear?

 Look at yourself in the mirror. Be quite honest and list your good points, figurewise, that you would choose to emphasize.
Then list the points that you are not so keen on which you would like to keep quiet.
Now, list the colours that you think you could wear. Think about your complexion, colour, and shape.
Look through a catalogue and cut out clothes that you would buy. Beside each item give a reason why you think it is suitable for you. □

 Have a look at these pictures of people. Choose one person and give your advice on the types of clothes which would suit them best. □

Another look at this unit

1 We wear clothes for many reasons: to make us feel and look attractive, to keep up warm and dry, to protect us, and to make us feel comfortable.
2 Knowing your bust/chest, waist, and hip measurements is very helpful when buying clothes. Buy 'top-half' clothes according to bust/chest size and 'bottom-half' clothes according to waist/hip size.
3 Think about your body shape and colouring when buying clothes. Use colour, line, pattern, and texture to your advantage.
4 Emphasize your good points with accessories such as badges, necklaces, belts, scarves.
5 Keep the receipt and care labels when you buy clothes – you never know when you might need them!

UNIT 11

The DIY clothes section

Do it yourself

When you have got some confidence in using the sewing machine how about having a go at making some clothes for yourself? Sometimes making your own clothes can work out cheaper than buying them ready-made. Many people enjoy making their own clothes: they get a lot of satisfaction, and it means they can make something that will fit properly and is not found in the shops.

The more garment construction you do, the more confident you will become. Therefore, it is best to try out your skills on something quite simple first. Pattern manufacturers do make 'very simple' or 'easy' patterns which are a good starting point.

Buying a pattern

Always buy the pattern before you buy the fabric. This is because the pattern will tell you how much fabric to buy. When you choose a pattern, think about all the points mentioned in Unit 10 about figure types. Buy a pattern for your size (see Unit 10 p. 66 for taking measurements). If you fall between two sizes then buy the one which is slightly larger. It is easier to take patterns in than to let them out. Also, buy a well-known make. Choose from the large catalogues in some department stores and specialist fabric shops.

Once you have found the pattern you like, give the assistant the make, number, and size you require. There are also patterns for girls, boys, children, and babies. Patterns are expensive so if you can find a friend who is the same size and who likes the same pattern as you, then why not share the pattern? Also, have a look at patterns which include several garments that you could make to get your money's worth.

Buy patterns in the same way as you would buy clothes, i.e. buy the 'top half' garments by bust or chest measurement (except for men's shirts which go on neck measurement), and the 'bottom half' garments by waist or hip measurement.

What your pattern tells you

Having got your pattern have a good look at the outside and see if you can see the following on the front:

7818
SIZE SM (32-34)
Simplicity®
0 39363 00084
PATTERN/PATRON
1
2
2
3
3
pattern number
figure type
size
make of pattern

And now on the back:

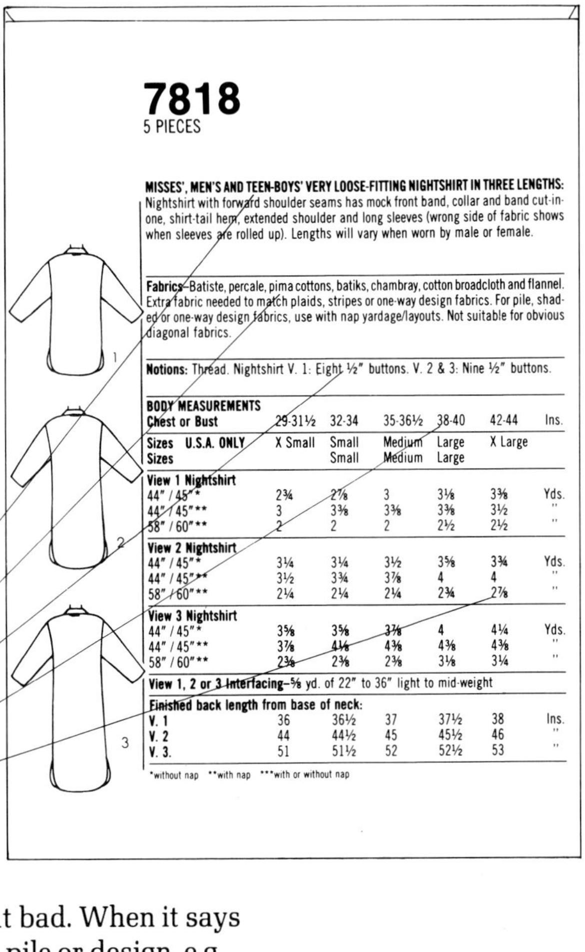
description of items
suggested fabrics for making the garment
haberdashery or extras required to complete the garment
standard body measurements
fabric amounts required for various views
1
2
3

7818
5 PIECES

MISSES', MEN'S AND TEEN-BOYS' VERY LOOSE-FITTING NIGHTSHIRT IN THREE LENGTHS: Nightshirt with forward shoulder seams has mock front band, collar and band cut-in-one, shirt-tail hem, extended shoulder and long sleeves (wrong side of fabric shows when sleeves are rolled up). Lengths will vary when worn by male or female.

Fabrics–Batiste, percale, pima cottons, batiks, chambray, cotton broadcloth and flannel. Extra fabric needed to match plaids, stripes or one-way design fabrics. For pile, shaded or one-way design fabrics, use with nap yardage/layouts. Not suitable for obvious diagonal fabrics.

Notions: Thread. Nightshirt V. 1: Eight ½" buttons. V. 2 & 3: Nine ½" buttons.

BODY MEASUREMENTS						
Chest or Bust	29-31½	32-34	35-36½	38-40	42-44	Ins.
Sizes U.S.A. ONLY	X Small	Small	Medium	Large	X Large	
Sizes		Small	Medium	Large		
View 1 Nightshirt						
44" / 45"*	2¾	2⅞	3	3⅛	3⅜	Yds.
44" / 45"**	3	3⅜	3⅜	3⅜	3½	"
58" / 60"**	2	2	2	2½	2½	"
View 2 Nightshirt						
44" / 45"*	3¼	3¼	3½	3⅝	3¾	Yds.
44" / 45"**	3½	3¾	3⅞	4	4	"
58" / 60"**	2¼	2¼	2¼	2¾	2⅞	"
View 3 Nightshirt						
44" / 45"*	3⅝	3⅝	3⅞	4	4¼	Yds.
44" / 45"**	3⅞	4⅛	4⅜	4⅜	4⅜	"
58" / 60"**	2⅜	2⅜	2⅜	3⅛	3¼	"
View 1, 2 or 3 Interfacing–⅝ yd. of 22" to 36" light to mid-weight						
Finished back length from base of neck:						
V. 1	36	36½	37	37½	38	Ins.
V. 2	44	44½	45	45½	46	"
V. 3.	51	51½	52	52½	53	"

*without nap **with nap ***with or without nap

It may look a bit complicated but it really isn't that bad. When it says 'with nap' it means fabrics which have a one-way pile or design, e.g. cotton corduroy, acrylic fur, and cotton velvet. It means that the pattern pieces will all have to be laid in the same direction when cutting out to prevent the various pieces being in different shades. This is because the pile, when facing one way, is a slightly different shade than when it is facing the other way. So you have to buy more material if you are using this type of fabric.

Making sense of a pattern envelope

The pattern envelope on the previous page has been marked to show you how to read the amount of fabric you will need for a small size, using fabric of 150 cm width.

Using the pattern envelope illustrated try to answer the following questions:

1 What size of pattern would you buy to fit yourself?
2 What size of pattern would you buy if your chest size was 94 cm?
3 How much fabric would you buy to make up View Two in 90 cm wide fabric for a small size?
4 What is the finished back length for a large size in View One?
5 List the haberdashery items needed to complete the garment in View Two.
6 What fabrics does the manufacturer suggest you use to make up the nightshirt? □

Buying the fabric

Once you have bought your pattern and know how to read the pattern envelope, you are ready to buy the fabric for your garment. If you are baffled by the choice available look at the pattern for suggestions of fabrics, or ask the assistant for help.

Here are some things to remember when buying fabric:

1 The fabric should be suitable for you (see Unit 10 – figure types and colours).
2 Consider what other clothes it will go with.
3 The fabric should be suitable for the pattern, e.g. stretchy fabric is needed for tracksuit bottoms.
4 Note any care requirements (look at the end of the roll for these).
5 Think about the features of the pattern – does it require a stiff or soft fabric, will the pattern of the fabric hide any of the features of the paper pattern design?

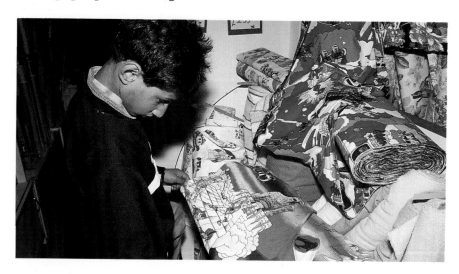

Now take a good look at the fabric:

How much does it cost and is it worth it?
Are there any flaws?
Will it stretch and recover? – Try it!
Is it soft or stiff?
Check the end of the roll for any pre-shrinking (especially for cottons).
Will it be rough or smooth next to the skin?
Does it crease? – Try it!
Look at the fibre content – will it be warm or cool to wear (see Unit 2)?
Is it absorbent?
Is it colour-fast? (If in doubt – ask!)

Buying the haberdashery

'Haberdashery' is the extra bits you need to complete your garment.
Try to buy this with the fabric so you can get a good match.

Thread   Different fabrics made from different fibres need different
types of thread (see Unit 8 p. 50).

Buttons   You will need to think about the number, size, shape, type,
and whether you need buttons with or without a shank.

Interfacing   This is the fabric used to stiffen or strengthen the
garment fabric in certain areas, for example in the waistband of
trousers or skirts, and for collars and cuffs on a blouse or shirt. You
need to think about:
- its weight (it shouldn't be heavier than the garment fabric);
- its colour – charcoal for dark fabrics, white for pale fabrics;
- whether it is sew-in or iron-on. Sew-in is simply tacked into
  position before use. Follow the instructions for iron-on;
- whether it is woven or non-woven. Woven interfacing has to be cut
  on the same straight of the grain as the garment, whereas non-
  woven can be cut in any direction so it is more economical;
- whether it will withstand the same washing requirements as the
  fabric.
  Look on the back of the pattern envelope for the amount to buy.

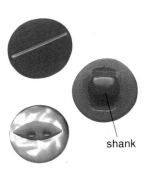

shank

Even more haberdashery

Zips   The things you need to think about here are the length, colour (background colour of the fabric if a printed fabric, darker colour if you can't find the exact match), open or closed end, and type (metal, nylon, jean, decorative).

Hooks and eyes or press studs   Buy silver/black if metal or white/transparent if plastic. Sizes range from 000 (very small) to 2.

Trims   Lace should if possible be made of the same fibres as the garment fabric. If you iron a cotton blouse trimmed with polyamide or nylon lace at the temperature required to iron cotton, the lace will melt.

Getting going!

You should now have everything you need to start your garment. Collect together all the equipment you will need as suggested in Unit 9 p. 55, including pins, needles, bobbin, tacking thread, a pin cushion, small scissors, and an unpicker. A sharp pair of cutting-out shears is essential – always buy the best quality you can afford.

Using the pattern

Inside the pattern you will find an instruction sheet. Don't, whatever you do, lose this, as it is your guide for cutting out and for making the garment.

1 Read the general instructions on how to use the pattern. Here is an example of an instruction sheet.

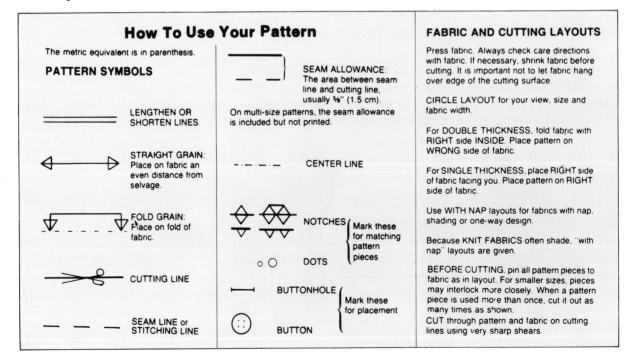

2 Each pattern piece has a letter or number on it so that you can find it easily. Look at the instruction sheet to help you. Select the pattern pieces needed for the view you are making. Cut round the pattern pieces just *outside* the solid block cutting line.

3 Check your body measurements against those in the pattern. Alter the pattern pieces if necessary *before* you cut out. The alteration lines on the pattern look like this:

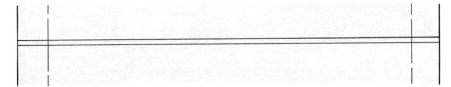

4 Find the correct pattern layout for the view you have chosen. Pin the pattern pieces on to the fabric according to the layout. Cut out the fabric with long even strokes using sharp scissors. Keep the fabric flat on the table. Cut round the *outside* of the little notches.

5 Transfer the important pattern markings used to make the garment on to the fabric. You can use tailor tacks, or dressmakers' carbon paper and a tracing wheel, or tailors' chalk, whatever you find the easiest (see Unit 9 p. 57).

6 Now just follow the instructions for making the garment, in the order they are given. You will find that the instructions have large, well-labelled diagrams which will help you by explaining what to do. The seam allowance, unless it says otherwise, is 15 cm. Always press the fabric as you go along for a more professional finish (see Unit 13).

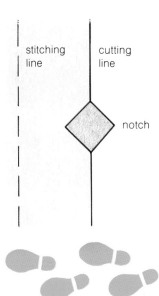

stitching line

cutting line

notch

Make a garment for yourself using a commercial paper pattern and a sewing machine. Use the Step-by-Step method to help you to decide what to do.□

Another look at this unit

1 Always buy the pattern before the fabric.
2 When buying the pattern consider your body shape and use a well-known make of pattern.
3 When buying fabric have a checklist of points to consider.
4 Try to buy all the haberdashery with the pattern and the fabric so you can match them exactly and easily.
5 Use the pattern instruction sheet to help you cut out and make the garment.
6 Finally, remember that practice makes perfect!

UNIT 12

Textiles all around us

Textiles in the home

A lot of people only think of textiles as clothing. They are quite surprised when you point out to them that textiles are all around us. You just have to look at your home to realize this (see Unit 1).

Textiles are being used more and more in the home to really good effect. It is up to you to create the atmosphere you want for each room and textiles can help to do this very well. How can you go about it?

Design dimensions

Imagine that you are fortunate enough to have the opportunity to decorate and re-equip a room, or all the rooms, in your home. To start with it is a good idea to plan each room as a separate unit. Think about the size and shape (dimensions) of each room. Does the room have any special features which you want to keep? Which direction does it face? This is important as it will tell you how much light and warmth it gets from the sun (facing south you get the most, facing north you get the least). You may need to use artificial lighting if the room is dark during the day. For each room, think about the furniture and floor covering you have already. Will it do or do you need something different? Can you afford it?

Decorating and furnishing even one room is very expensive. So it is worth spending as much time as you can deciding how you would like to change it to suit you and your family. As you are likely to have to live with the finished result for a long time, it is wise to choose carefully.

A splash of colour

Most people can tell you the colours in a room – it's one of the first things they notice. Here is a good chance, as with the clothes you wear, to show off your personality to people you invite into your home. But don't forget you will probably have to live with your choice longer than your visitors!

Colour can create a room's atmosphere and it can also kill it. Colour helps make a room seem dramatic or simple, restful or busy, warm or cool.

Have a look at the colour wheel in Unit 5 p. 30. You will see that the colours opposite each other are called **contrast colours**. When these are used together, for example red and green, you get a very dramatic effect in home decorating. However, contrasting colours can be very irritating if you have to live with them for any length of time. They can also make you feel restless if they are used in rooms where you are likely to sit or stay for some time. But you can use them in halls, on stairs or landings where you want to create a stunning effect, and you probably won't get irritated by them because you don't stay in these places for very long.

Let's have some harmony

The colours which are next to one another on the colour wheel are called **harmonious colours**. When used together in a room they give a very peaceful effect. You could use harmonious colours in living rooms and bedrooms with just a splash of contrasting colour to liven the place up a little.

By using warm colours such as reds, pinks, oranges, and yellows, you can create a very warm, cosy room. The only problem is that these colours tend to make rooms seem smaller. Greens, blues, and greys are cool colours and have the opposite effect by making a room feel larger. So if you have a small room you can make it seem larger by using cool colours. To make a room look larger you can also use pale colours in much the same way as clothing (see Unit 10 p. 68). Dark colours will make a room seem smaller.

Pattern preferences

It's up to people to choose how much pattern they want in a room. Indeed, some people may not want any pattern. However, pattern can be used to break up plain colours and add a little more interest to a room. Examples of patterns are books on a bookshelf, pictures on a wall, a bowl of fruit, a vase of flowers, patterned wallcoverings or curtains, and cushions on chairs.

Beware, though! Too much pattern can be confusing to the eye. If you plan carefully, patterns can be used to create interesting features to a room. It's up to you to decide.

Changing shape?

You can also alter the proportions of a room with pattern, in just the same way as you can with colours. If you use horizontal (going round) stripes, you can make a room seem smaller. Vertical (going up/down) stripes make the eye travel upwards and the room seems higher. Diagonal and zig-zag lines, when used in small amounts, can give an interesting and dramatic effect to a room. Curves make a room seem more soothing and restful.

 See if you can find an old wallpaper book.
Looking through the wallpaper book choose some designs which would look good in your bedroom.
Then choose some designs which would be suitable for a bathroom and a kitchen. □

Getting the right feel

The feel of a surface, or its texture, also helps to create the mood of a room. Texture doesn't really affect the apparent size of a room in the way that pattern and colour do. Like pattern, texture is used to add interest. Rough, chunky, textures, e.g. brickwork, soft rugs, velvet curtains, all give a feeling of warmth and cosiness. The cooler textures of chrome, brasswork, mirrors, gloss-painted woodwork, and glass all give a cooler appearance to a room and can make it more formal and elegant.

Warm textures

Cool textures

Remember, though, that the choice is yours. Think about the above points and look for ideas in magazines, books, and other people's homes. Choose really carefully to create the atmosphere and the effect you want.

 Imagine that you and your family have moved into a new house. Your room is to be the attic which is a bit dark and cold. The attic is large with plenty of room. How would you redecorate it? Draw a plan of the room – the size and shape is up to you. What colour scheme would you have? Draw on your plan the furniture you would like in your room. Explain how you would use pattern and texture to their full advantage. □

Furnishing a room

Textiles really come into their own when thinking about soft furnishings in the home. Soft furnishings are the extras that make rooms more comfortable, personal, and attractive. Fabrics for soft furnishings should be strong and long-lasting.

Curtains

Curtains help to keep a room warm by stopping draughts. They also give privacy. Curtains can be used to create pattern in a room by using a patterned fabric. They can also create a feeling of warmth if they are made from warm textured fabric, e.g. cotton velveteen. Smooth, shiny fabrics give an impression of coolness.

When buying curtains, or fabric to make your own, take into consideration how the manufacturer suggests you clean them. Dry cleaning for curtains is an expensive business. If you want to wash your curtains at home they should not shrink and they should also be colour-fast. If in doubt, ask the shop assistant.

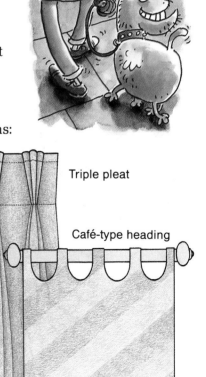

Curtains which are lined also help to keep draughts out better than unlined curtains. Lining also protects the curtain fabric if it is likely to fade in the sun. Curtains which are lined tend to hang a lot better because there is more weight to pull them down. If the lining is actually fixed to the curtain then check that the washing instructions for the lining are similar to those for the curtain fabric.

Net curtains are also useful as they give extra privacy without blocking out the light. You buy them according to the length or amount of 'drop' you need. So measure carefully from where the net curtains are to hang to the length you would like.

Fabrics suitable for curtains are cottons and cotton blends, polyamide, polyester, acrylic, and acrylic blends. To add even more fun there are many types of headings which you can use for curtains:

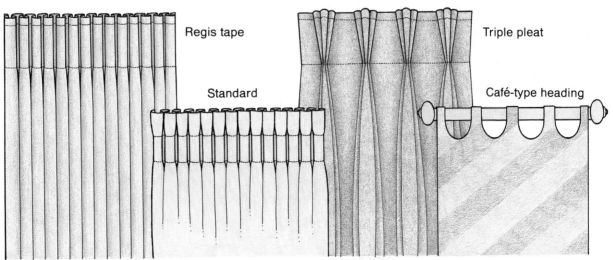

Regis tape

Standard

Triple pleat

Café-type heading

Turning a blind eye!

Blinds are a good idea for windows where you want different amounts of light to come in at different times of the day. Blinds can be decorative or plain. They can be used at a window by themselves or with curtains in a contrasting or matching fabric. Choose between Roller and Austrian blinds if you want to have a go at making them yourself.

Sitting down on it

Fabrics for upholstery are expensive, so it is important to choose these with care. The most important thing is that this type of fabric should be comfortable and hardwearing. Check to see that it is stain resistant and easy to clean. Patterned and textured fabrics show the dirt less than plain fabrics. Seat covers which can be removed for cleaning are useful if there are small children and pets around.

Loose covers can be made to cover old or worn furniture, or if you decide you would like a new colour scheme. You can make your own, have them made to measure, or buy them ready-made. Fabrics suitable for upholstery include leather, imitation leather, dralon, viscose weaves, wool and wool blends, and heavyweight cottons.

Cushioning the blow!

Cushions add interest, pattern, and texture to a room. They can be any shape or size you wish, from large floor cushions to small decorative ones. Their main function is to give comfort and support while sitting down. They also add colour to a room by either blending in with the existing colour or by creating a contrast effect. They are costly to buy but relatively inexpensive to make.

Any fabric can be used according to the effect you want to create, but do consider the weight and fibre content of the fabric. Cushions can be made more interesting by adding some form of decoration to them, such as appliqué, quilting, tucks, or embroidery.

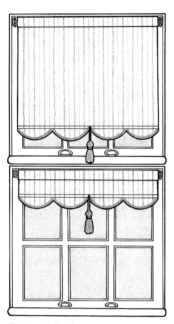
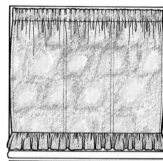
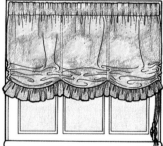

Roller blinds

Austrian blinds

 Have a go at designing your own personalized cushion cover. When you have done this, why not make it? □

All lit up!

Lighting is an important feature of a room. Lamps and fittings should suit the atmosphere of the room. They add extra dimensions to the overall scheme of a room by emphasizing specific areas or objects, in much the same way as accessories do for clothing. As a general rule use light colours for reading and studying and darker colours for a more relaxing or dramatic effect.

 Find an old catalogue. Cut out pictures of three different types of lighting and beside each one say where you would use this form of lighting and why. □

Why is table-linen called linen?

Table-linen is so called because it was originally made from the fibre linen or flax. The problem is that this fibre is quite expensive and difficult to look after, although it does look very nice. Nowadays, easy-care fabrics are used, such as cotton and polyester, which are available in many different sizes, shapes, colours, patterns, and designs.

Creating your own

Table-cloths, table-mats and napkins/serviettes are expensive to buy but you can make your own. In this way they will be far more individual. Scalloping the edge of a table-cloth, quilting tie-and-dye table-mats, or using appliqué round the edges of a round table-cloth all add an extra bit of something.

Fabric for sleeping on

Sheets can be bought in two widths, 230 cm (for double beds) and 178 cm (for single beds). Suitable fabric, such as pure cotton or polyester and cotton (this is easier to look after and is used by most manufacturers), comes in a wide variety of colours and prints. It can be bought to mix and match with curtains and wall coverings. You can buy flat or fitted bottom sheets. Some come with valances attached.

Fabric for sleeping under

Duvet covers can be bought to match the bottom sheet and pillowcases. Again, these can be made quite easily. Duvets themselves have a tog rating – the higher the tog rating the warmer they will be. They are filled with either feathers, feathers and down, or polyester.

The warmest blankets are those made of wool which are difficult to care for and should be moth-proofed. Acrylic, wool blends, acrylic blends, polyamide, and viscose are all used for blankets. Bed spreads or bed covers can be bought in different fabrics and styles. But do think about the washing needed and the wearing ability before buying.

 What bedding would you have in the attic room you designed on p. 78? Look at some catalogues to get some ideas.
How much will your choice cost? □

Some extras

Small items like mixer covers, drinks mats, tool holders, tissue-box covers, and mirror and picture frames can be made to give a room a feeling of 'completeness'. They can also be fiddly but are useful presents.

 Make an item which can be used in your home and which involves some form of decorative work. □

Another look at this unit

1 Use textiles to show off your taste and personality in the home.
2 Consider colour, pattern, and texture when redecorating a room.
3 Soft furnishings can be expensive to buy and much cheaper to make. But don't tackle something too difficult – it's false economy if you have to pay someone to finish it for you.
4 When buying fabrics for soft furnishings be sure they are strong and hardwearing.

UNIT 13

Looking after textiles: keeping them clean

Dust and dirt

Dust and dirt are annoying facts of life. Textile items are no exception. All of them, at some stage, will get dirty. This unit is a basic guide to use when trying to get items clean. The idea is to get items clean with as little damage as possible. Because there are so many different fabrics on the market it is impossible to give anything other than general advice.

General care

As most items are expensive a little thought given to their care isn't a bad idea. Try to hang clothes up or fold them neatly – not always easy but it does help. If a garment is a little creased you can always give it a quick press with an iron. This should revive it, provided it isn't too dirty or smelly!

Dashing away with a smoothing iron!

Be careful about these points when you are using an iron:
1 Don't store it with the flex wrapped around it when it is hot. Empty it of water if it is a steam iron.
2 Store it in a dry place away from children.
3 Don't leave it switched on unused for any length of time as the thermostat will be ruined.
4 Don't iron over anything that will scratch the sole plate as this may snag fabrics.
5 Keep the sole plate clean and shiny.
6 Have the flex and plug checked by an electrician if you are unsure whether the iron is safe to use or not.

Getting the sole plate to the fabric

When using an iron, always set it to the temperature suitable for the fabric being ironed or pressed (see p. 86). When pressing fabric the iron is pressed down heavily in one place, lifted, and then pressed down in another place, and so on. Ironing is when the iron slides over the fabric, smoothing out creases on the right side of the fabric.

A few extras

There are several other pieces of pressing equipment which may be useful when making and caring for clothes. For example:

A damp **pressing cloth** makes pressing more effective if you are using a dry iron. Muslin and cheesecloth are good fabrics to use as you can see through them, but an old tea-towel will do just as well. Work from the wrong side of the fabric and try not to over-press as the fabric will go shiny!

A **sleeveboard** looks like a small ironing board and is designed to fit on top of one. It is useful for pressing the seams of sleeves and trousers, as well as necklines and sleeve heads during garment construction.

A pressing tip!

If you press seams from the wrong side and the imprint of the seam allowance shows on the right side, try inserting a piece of brown paper between the seam and the garment to prevent this from happening. Always make sure that you set the iron to the fabric temperature suitable for the fabric.

Careful pressing during and after making a textile item will give it a more professional look.

Getting rid of those stains

At some time you might get a stain on your clothes. It is important that you do something about it straight away, otherwise it is likely to leave a mark. If the item is washable, rinse the stained area in cold water – hot water may 'set' the stain. Then soak it in a washing or biological powder. Soaking gives the powder a chance to act on the stain. Follow this by washing it in the recommended way.

Bleaching it out

Bleaches can be used to remove stains from small areas, e.g. spots. But check first to see if the care label says 'do not bleach' (⚠)! Make up $\frac{1}{2}$ fluid ounce of bleach to 2 pints of cold water. Place a clean absorbent cloth below the spot and dab the stain with another cloth. Rinse thoroughly in cold water and then wash. If it is a large area that is stained, use $\frac{1}{2}$ fluid ounce to $2\frac{1}{2}$ gallons of cold water. Soak the article for 10–15 minutes. Rinse thoroughly and then wash.

ALWAYS check the label for colour fastness and rinse thoroughly after the treatment. This is particularly important for dark and brightly-coloured fabrics which may have to be washed on their own a few times.

NEVER use undiluted bleach or have naked skin near the bleach as it burns. Never use bleach on silk, wool, or flame-resistant fabric because it will ruin them.

Dissolving it out

Solvents are used on stains which are greasy, grease-based, or oily. Solvents are trichlorethylene (sold under many trade names), turpentine, methylated spirits (surgical spirit), and acetone. Remove the soiled matter carefully. Place an absorbent cloth underneath the stain. Soak another cloth in the solvent and dab in a circle, starting from the outside of the stain and working your way into the centre. Rinse thoroughly and wash normally. If the item is not washable make sure that you air it thoroughly.

ALWAYS check for colour fastness and rinse or air thoroughly after treatment.

NEVER use in a closed room – make sure that the room is well ventilated. Never use near a naked flame because solvents ignite very easily. Never use acetone on acetate as it will dissolve it! You can also use ammonia (be careful), acetic acid (vinegar), salt, fat, and lemon juice on stains.

A stain removal guide

> **Egg, coffee, milk, perspiration, blood, tea** Brush off any hardened bits and wash in a biological powder.
>
> **Beer** Wash or dab with 1 part vinegar to 4 parts water and rinse thoroughly.
>
> **Grease, oil** Scrape off as much as you can and then wash at the highest possible temperature. Treat with a solvent and then rinse and air.
>
> **Ballpoint pen** Dab with methylated spirits, then air and wash.
>
> **Ink** Cover the stain with salt. Then put lemon juice on the salt and leave it for an hour rinse and wash.
>
> **Emulsion (wall) paint** Treat straight away with cold water.
>
> **Oil paint** Dab with white spirit or solvent and wash.
>
> **Chewing gum** Place in the freezer and pick off when frozen.

If you don't know what the stain is, then take the item to the dry cleaners. Tell them how long the stain has been there and what you have done, if anything, to remove it.

Getting rid of that stain

🔍 Have a look at home and see if you can find any textile items with stains on them. Choose one which you can bring into school. Have a go at removing the stain. How successful were you? ☐

🔍 Find two, fairly large, scraps of the same fabric and do your own staining! Stain both pieces of fabric with the same stains.
Try chewing gum (great fun!), grass, coffee, red wine (for spilling not drinking!), blood (ooch!), and ballpoint pen.
Try removing the stains on one piece of fabric straight away.
How successful were you?
Now try removing the stains on the other piece of fabric once they have set (you can tell this because they will be dry).
How successful were you?
Is it easier to remove stains before or after they have set? ☐

Reading the label

Whenever you want to clean textile items, always check the label on the item first. As a result of the International Textile Care Labelling Code (ITCLC) the majority of garments and household items have a label which gives you full instructions on: washing ⊔ bleaching △ , ironing ⊿ , drying ▢ , and dry cleaning ○ .

What the label tells you

Here is a summary of the washing symbols that you will find on labels:

Bleaching △ this fabric can withstand chlorine bleach

△ do not bleach

Ironing ⊿ hot (210°C) – viscose rayon, modified rayon, cotton, and linen

⊿ warm (160°C) – polyester mixtures and wool

⊿ cool (120°C) – acrylics, polyamide, acetate, rayon, and polyester

⊿ do not iron

Taking it to the cleaners

Here is a guide for commercial dry-cleaners, but do check the fluid in coin-operated machines:

Ⓐ all solvents may be used

(P) perchlorethylene, white spirit solvent, solvent 113, or solvent 11 may be used

(F) white spirit or solvent 113 can be used

⊗ do not dry-clean

Drying symbols:

▣ tumble-drying O.K.

⊠ do not tumble-dry

|||| drip dry

☐ line dry

⊟ dry flat

A commercial dry-cleaning machine

Wool symbols

Wool is regarded as a fabric which needs extra care in cleaning. The labels will indicate hand wash only, dry clean, or machine wash (super-wash):

PURE NEW WOOL MACHINE WASHABLE

Certification Trade Mark
Wool rich blend

Certification Trade Mark
Pure new wool

It is much safer to hand wash or dry clean a woollen item if you are not sure what to do.

 The ITCLC symbols can be found on the side of all washing powder packets.
Using a washing powder packet to help you, draw the type of care label you would expect to find on the following textile items:
a polycotton shirt; **b** wool jumper; **c** bath towel;
d nylon sheet; **e** bedroom curtains.
Now look at the labels on these items and see what the manufacturer suggested. How close were you? □

Before washing

When sorting through a pile of washing, those items with similar care labels can be washed together. Items of a dark or a bright colour may still run, so beware. Empty all pockets, secure fastenings, try to remove any stains and check for any repairs needed before washing.

Checking out the label

Have a look at the labels on some of the garments you are wearing.
Draw these labels and beside each one explain what it means.
Which garments would you wash together? □

A little powder goes a long way

There are many different washing powders available today. It's
important to have a good look at the packet first so you know what
you are buying and what to use the powder for.

There are three main types of powder:
1 **Soap powders**   These can form a scum in hard water. They
   should never be used on flame resistant fabric because the soap
   forms a flammable layer on the finish of the fabric.
2 **Synthetic washing powders**   These lather well and don't produce
   any scum. They also work well at all temperatures.
3 **Biological powders**   The biological part is the enzymes. Enzymes
   are pretty powerful chemical substances which speed up various
   chemical reactions in plants and animals. Manufacturers put
   enzymes in washing powders because they remove stains by
   breaking them down. Enzymes work well at 40°C because this is
   the temperature at which they can do their work most efficiently.

There are also washing powders designed specifically for automatic
washing machines. These make very little lather. It's not a good idea
to use ordinary washing powder in an automatic washing machine –
it will make rather too much lather!

Getting things clean

Three things are needed to remove dirt from fabrics – water,
detergent, and agitation. Together they wet and loosen dirt.

To see how water, detergent, and agitation work together to wet
fabric you will need:
a watch glass filled with water, two needles, a pipette filled with
washing-up liquid.
Place the needles on the water and see what happens.
Add two drops of washing-up liquid – what happens? ■

It's all to do with tension

When you put a needle on water it will float because it is held there by the surface tension of the water. The surface tension of the water is rather like a skin. When you add the detergent the surface tension is greatly weakened which allows the needle to drop to the bottom.

When you wet fabric you get exactly the same effect. It is very difficult to get fabric really wet without a lot of agitation because of surface tension. The water is only too happy to roll up in little balls on the fabric. Unless the water gets right into the fabric there is no way that you are going to get it clean. So, this is one job that a detergent does – it helps to make the fabric really wet all the way through.

Water-loving or water-hating?

The other job detergent does is to loosen dirt. A tiny piece of a detergent (a molecule) has a water-loving end and a water-hating end.

The tails simply hate water so they bury themselves in the dirt or grease on the fabric. This leaves the heads, which so love water they can't get enough of it, sticking out. In this way they get a firm grip on the dirt.

With a little agitation

To get rid of the dirt you have to help the detergent to move the dirt. This is done with some agitation. The lumps of dirt and grease float out of the fabric and won't return because there are all those water-loving heads sticking out of it and they don't want to get involved with any more fabric, thank you very much! Also the place where the dirt has come from is taken with more detergent so there is no way back. The water with the dirt in it is then rinsed away, leaving the fabric clean.

 See if you can explain the following.
You will need:
two test tubes, a test tube holder, cooking oil in a pipette, and washing-up liquid in a pipette.

Half fill the test tubes with water.
Add five drops of oil to each test tube.
Add five drops of washing-up liquid to only one test tube.
Shake both test tubes well.
Leave to stand for five minutes and note what happens.
Why does this happen? ■

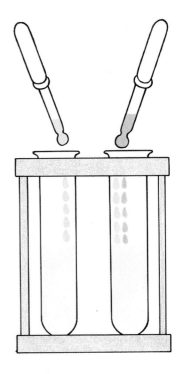

Dry-cleaning

Some items should be dry-cleaned. Remember to check and empty pockets and to do any repairs before taking an item to be dry cleaned. Some dry-cleaners are members of a professional association, 'The Association of British Launderers and Cleaners', or ABLC. Those which have this sign in their window will guarantee certain standards, known as a Code of Practice as agreed with the Office of Fair Trading. This does not apply to coin-operated dry-cleaners though.

You can take items either to a dry-cleaners and leave them there to collect later, or to a launderette which has a coin-operated dry-cleaning machine which you operate yourself. If you go for a do-it-yourself job, follow the instructions on the machine and don't be tempted to overload it.

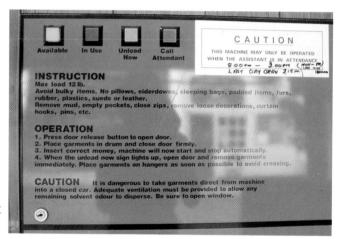

 How many dry-cleaners are there in your nearest town?
How many of these dry-cleaners are members of the ABLC?
How much does it cost to clean a winter coat at one of these dry-cleaners? ∎

Another look at this unit

1 Take care when choosing the best method for cleaning an item. The idea is that it should be cleaned with as little damage as possible to the item's appearance and properties.
2 Every item should have a care label attached to it. Follow these instructions and you shouldn't go far wrong.
3 In stain removal, prompt action is important before the stain penetrates the fabric. Take care when using bleaches and solvents.
4 When doing a lot of washing, collect items with similar care labels so that you can wash them together.

UNIT 14

Looking after textiles: running repairs

Most clothes and textile items are fairly expensive. They also need repairing from time to time so it's worth knowing how to do this.

Doing it up

Sometimes fastenings just fall off after lots of use or if they have been put under too much strain!

Button and buttonholes Let's take a look at buttons first. Buttons can fall off easily, especially on some shop-bought items. If you have lost a button, try to get an exact replacement or you will have to buy enough buttons to change the whole lot – unless you don't mind having one odd button!

Buttons without a shank (a stem under the button and between the fabric), i.e. flat buttons, should be sewn on with thread that matches the colour of the button, as it will show. If the fabric has been torn, then place a piece of interfacing between the fabrics to strengthen them and hand-stitch the fabric to the interfacing.

If you follow these instructions for sewing on a button you will have to pull really hard before it will come off again:
On the underside of the fabric work a double backstitch to start off. Position the button and pass the needle through the holes in the button. Do not pull the button to the fabric too tightly as you will need to form a shank so that the top layer with the buttonhole can stay fastened without pulling.

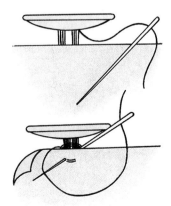

Having sewn the button in position, pass the needle through the holes at least six times. Take the thread through one of the holes so that it is between the button and the fabric and wind it round the button threads to form a stem or shank. Take the thread through to the wrong side and blanket stitch neatly over the threads. Cast off. Don't bother making a shank if your button already has one.

What about buttonholes?

These sometimes get frayed from a lot of use. If this happens it's worth cutting off the frayed bits. Then set the machine to close satin stitch (stitch length nearly 0, stitch width 3, needle position centre), and zig-zag round the buttonhole with thread that is suited to the fabric and the colour of the item. Or you can buttonhole stitch by hand over the frayed places.

Other fastenings which don't take the strain!

Zips The teeth can become loose and then you can't do the zip up. If this happens it is best to take the whole zip out and put another one in. Sometimes the waistband, or the top of the zip facing, may have to be unpicked a little to get the zip out. Use an unpicker to do this and be careful not to tear the fabric. Use a zipper foot on a sewing machine to help get the new zip in. It is usually easier to stitch one side in first and then the other side. Make sure you secure all thread ends.

Hooks and eyes and press studs All of these can be pulled off. Again, if the fabric is frayed, place a small piece of interfacing between the layers and hand sew as invisibly as possible in place. Use thread which is suitable for the colour and fibre content of the fabric. Sew the fastener in position. Oversewing is the easiest stitch to use when sewing hooks and eyes and press studs on, but buttonhole stitch is much, much stronger.

Using buttonhole stitch

Using oversewing stitch

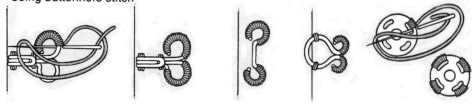

Splitting your sides!

If you split a seam then unpick the seam until the thread ends are long enough to weave in and out of the machine stitching. Pull the ends through to the same side and weave in and out as shown in the diagram:

Use thread suitable for the fibre content and colour of the fabric. Set the machine (stitch length $2\frac{1}{2}$ and width 0). Stitch along the seam line and secure the ends.

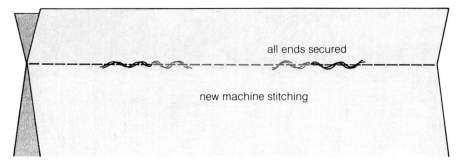

all ends secured

new machine stitching

Mending hems

If it is a case of simply hand sewing then you can either slip hem if the hem has a fold or hem it in place if there isn't a fold:

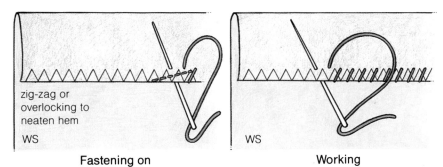

zig-zag or
overlocking to
neaten hem

WS

WS

Fastening on

Working

If you aren't very keen on hand sewing then you can use a little strip of interfacing-type fabric which has adhesive on both sides of it. The adhesive will stick to the garment on one side and to the hem on the other – clever stuff! Either follow the manufacturer's instructions, or:

1 Insert the tape between the hem and the garment.
2 Dampen a lightweight cloth (e.g. a large handkerchief) and lay this on top of the hem).
3 Set the iron to a heat which is suitable for the fabric.
4 Work round the hemline using a pressing action. Make sure that the cloth protects the fabric and check between each press that the fabric isn't puckered.

You can also buy sheets of this sticky fabric for making appliqué designs (see Unit 9 p. 60).

A right old rip!

It's really annoying when you tear an item. The best way of dealing with tears or rips is with a swing-needle sewing machine. Follow these instructions:

1 Cut a piece of interfacing (lighter in weight than the actual fabric), large enough to cover the tear completely.
2 On the wrong side, tack the interfacing into position if it is the sew-on type, or use a damp cloth and iron it on.
3 Thread the machine with suitable thread. Set the machine to stitch length nearly 0, stitch width 3–4, needle position centre.
4 Simply zig-zag over the tear, working several overlapping rows if necessary. Be sure to cover the tear completely.
5 On the wrong side, trim the interfacing down to the stitching. The finished item should look like this:

work from the right side

RS

WS

Doing your own repairs

Have a look at home to see if you can find any clothing in need of repair. Have a go at repairing it using this unit to help you. You could be the family's favourite person! □

Patching it up

If you have got a hole in a woven fabric then you can put a patch on the top of the hole to cover it. Again you can use the swing needle machine and suitable thread. The method is very similar to that used when working appliqué (see Unit 9 p. 60).

1 If you think the hole will fray, zig-zag round it first (stitch length 1, stitch width 3, and needle position centre).
2 Cut the patch – a square or oblong – large enough to cover the hole, plus an extra 1 cm all round. Make sure that the straight of the grain runs in the same direction and match any patterns if you can. Use fabric from hems if you haven't got any spare pieces.
3 Pin and tack the patch in place on the right side.
4 Straight stitch (stitch length $2\frac{1}{2}$, stitch width 0, needle position centre) round the hole, forming a square. Make sure that there is at least 5 mm of patch fabric away from the edge of the hole.
5 Trim the fabric down to the straight stitching.
6 Satin stitch round the patch (stitch length nearly 0, stitch width 3–4, needle position centre). All corners should be covered.

Creative patches can be made using free machine embroidery on the patches before stitching them in position. They can be of various shapes but do try to match the straight of the grain of the patch to that of the item.

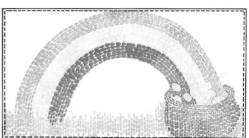

 Make a pair of dungarees for a small child featuring a decorative patch pocket on the bib and extra decorative patches on the knees.☐

Another look at this unit

1 If you rip or wear away your clothes or any textile item, try to mend them straight away before they get any worse.
2 For all repairs, use thread which is suited to the fibre content and the colour of the fabric to be repaired.
3 Frayed buttonholes can be zig-zagged to prevent them fraying even more.
4 Hems can be hemmed, slip-hemmed, or stuck up with adhesive tape.
5 An effective way of mending tears is to zig-zag over them carefully with a piece of interfacing on the wrong side for support.
6 Patches and darns can be worked using the swing needle machine which saves time. Patches and darns done in this way are very strong and hardwearing.

HAVE FUN!

Index

absorbency   8, 10, 14–16, 22, 32, 33, 44, 73, 84, 85
acrylics   12, 13, 15, 45, 71, 79, 82, 86
appliqué   60, 61, 80, 81, 94

beetling   41, 45
blending   16, 20, 28
body measurements   65, 66, 69, 71, 75
body shape   67, 69, 75
bonded fibre fabric   25, 28
buttons   73, 91, 92, 95

calendering   41, 45
care labels   84–8, 90
colour   29–37, 40, 41, 57, 60, 67–9, 72–4, 77, 78, 80–2, 87, 91–3, 95
   contrast   30, 35, 77
   harmonious   77
   primary   29, 30, 35
   secondary   29, 30, 35
   shade   30
   tertiary   30, 35
   tint   30
cotton   11–17, 20, 31, 33, 37, 41–5, 50, 56, 59–61, 63, 71, 73, 74, 79–81, 86, 87
crease holding   9, 15, 45
crease resistant   9, 15, 16, 45
curtains   77–81, 87
cushions   77, 80

darns   95
dry cleaning   86, 87, 90
dyeing   31–9
   commercial   32, 34
   mordant   33
   natural   32–4
   resist   34, 35

embroidery   56, 58–61, 63, 80, 95
enzymes   88
equipment   55, 84
   irons   40, 61, 74, 83, 84, 86, 93, 94
      sleeveboard   84

felt   25, 28
fibres   9–14, 16–21, 25, 28, 31–3, 35, 41, 43–5, 50, 60, 73, 80, 81, 92, 93, 95
   continuous   11, 12, 14, 17
   man-made   12, 16, 17

natural   11, 12, 16, 20, 32
staple   11, 12, 14, 17
synthetic   12, 16, 17, 20, 32
finishes   31, 33, 37, 41–5, 88
flame-proofing   42, 45, 85, 88
flammability   9, 42, 88
flax   11, 17, 81

haberdashery   71–5
hardwearing   9, 10, 15, 41, 79, 80, 95
heatset   9, 15, 20, 45
hooks and eyes   74, 92

interfacing   61, 73, 93–5
ITCLC   86, 87

patches   94, 95
patterns   65, 70–5
pile   22
planning   26–8, 76–8
ply   19
polyamides   12, 13, 15, 41, 45, 74, 79, 82, 86
   nylon   12, 15, 34, 43, 74, 87
polyester   12–16, 20, 33, 45, 59, 61, 79, 81, 82, 86, 87
printing   31–9
   block   36, 37, 40
   screen   39, 40
   spraying   38
   stencilling   38, 40
   transfer   40
problem-solving   26
properties   9, 14–16, 20, 90

quilting   61–3, 80

rayon   12, 13, 41–5, 86
   acetate   12, 13, 42, 85, 86
   triacetate   12
   viscose   12–14, 32, 33, 41, 42, 45, 80, 82, 86
repairs   91, 94, 95

selvedge   22
sewing machine   46–8, 50–4, 59, 60, 62, 63, 70, 75, 92–5
   needles   46–51, 53, 54, 62, 63, 92–4
   stitches   46–9, 51–4, 58–60, 62, 63, 92–4

shrinkage   9, 43, 45, 73
silk   11, 13, 14, 17, 36, 50, 85
soft furnishings   79, 82
spinning   12, 17, 18, 20, 25
stain resistant   9, 44, 45, 80
stains   84–8, 90
static electricity   15
step-by-step   26, 28, 35, 40, 53, 59, 63, 75, 82, 95
surface tension   89

texturing   20, 79, 80
thermoplastic   20, 45
threads/yarns   9, 16–21, 23–5, 28, 31, 32, 46–8, 50–9, 61–3, 73, 74, 91–5
trubenizing   41, 45

warp   21, 22, 28
washing powders   84, 85, 87–9
water repellent   44, 45, 89
weaving   21, 22, 25, 28, 44, 80
weft   21, 22, 28
wool   11, 13–15, 17–19, 28, 41–5, 50, 56, 80, 82, 85–7

zips   74, 92